There are people who walk into your life and quietly, profoundly change its course. Richard Ashworth is one of those people for me. As my mentor in Feng Shui and Chinese Astrology, Richard did more than teach me systems, charts, and formulas. He opened a doorway to a deeper world, one where energy moves with intention, where spaces speak, and where our destiny can be understood not with fear but with clarity and purpose.

**Janine Lowe,** author of the best-selling *Feng Shui Your Way to Abundance* and *Date, Love, Marry, Avoid*

# What People Are Saying About
# Author Richard Ashworth

I never fail to be astonished by Richard's relentless and dedicated quest to unravel the secrets of the Ba Zi. His research has taken him to many parts of the globe, to learn from traditional masters and, in turn, to share his discoveries with them. Few, if any, Western teachers would surpass his knowledge of this particular field of Chinese traditional culture.
**Derek Walters,** author of the *Complete Guide to Chinese Astrology*

Richard's brand of feng shui is not about your curtains; this guy tackles your personal issues in a way that inspires both confidence and awe in equal measure. He partners you through this process of self-exploration and growth and leads you out the other side with demons conquered, life issues resolved. WARNING: he may make you cry.
**Gillian Anderson,** *The X Files*, *Sex Education*, and *The Crown*

Richard Ashworth is a superb teacher, he has developed a number of courses which lead to a comprehensive mastery of the foundations of classical Chinese metaphysics, and lead to an in depth understanding and proficiency in these astonishing and complex arts. I recommend starting with Ba Zi – you will learn to hand-draft in Classical Chinese – an essential and overlooked part of the divination process which will also allow English speakers to go on to learn with Chinese masters who generally do not use the animal zodiac. It also provides the foundations for his Feng Shui courses.
**Ryan Terren,** Qi Gung and Tai Chi Master

I love his wit, wisdom and insights which combine with his amazing knowledge to provide entertaining and resourceful information.
**Jon Sandifer,** author of *Feng Shui Astrology*

Your advice to me as to precisely when the downturn would occur and when it would pick up was bang on.
**Naomie Harris,** Academy Award nominee, *Skyfall, Pirates of the Caribbean, Small Island*

Richard is a scholar with a thirst for knowledge, superb consultant and healer who genuinely cares about his clients, successful media presenter and exemplary parent, all of which he manages with unassuming modesty and a wicked sense of fun.
**Gill Hale,** author of *The Feng Shui Encyclopedia*.

Richard is the man I trust with my own space.
**Kelly Hoppen,** International Designer, *Dragons' Den*

With this new book, Richard Ashworth offers an enlightening convergence of ancient Chinese wisdom and human nature. His approach is both innovating and intriguing. This is another valuable, authentic contribution in English by one of the pioneers in the application of ancient Chinese Metaphysics in the Western world.
**Dr. Simona Mainini,** ***Dr. Arch.,*** feng shui master, author, and founder of Feng Shui for Architecture Training Center

# I Talk to the Animals

## A Definitive Guide to the Four Pillars of Destiny

# I Talk to the Animals

## A Definitive Guide to the Four Pillars of Destiny

Richard Ashworth

BOOKS

London, UK
Washington, DC, USA

CollectiveInk

First published by O-Books, 2025
O-Books is an imprint of Collective Ink Ltd.,
Unit 11, Shepperton House, 89 Shepperton Road, London, N1 3DF
office@collectiveinkbooks.com
www.collectiveinkbooks.com
www.o-books.com

For distributor details and how to order, please visit the 'Ordering' section on our website.



ISBN: 978 1 80341 899 5
978 1 80341 933 6 (ebook)
Library of Congress Control Number: 2024944519



A CIP catalogue record for this book is available from the British Library.

Design: Lapiz Digital Services
Cover art by Ellie Spinelli
Circular drawing in Module II provided by Nancy Canestaro
Jack Chiu calendar reproduced by permission of its author

UK: Printed and bound by CPI Group (UK) Ltd, Croydon, CR0 4YY
Printed in North America by CPI GPS partners

# Chapter Listing



**A Note About Chinese Characters**: There are two recognised ways of turning the pronunciation of Chinese Characters into European lettering. These are Wade Giles – from which we get "Peking", and Pin Yin which renders the same word "Beijing". In my experience neither method is 100% reliable for Ba Zi terminology. To complicate the issue my first teacher, Grand Master Chan Kun Wah, was no great respecter of either. And so, many of the terms I use are the specialised Cantonese in which he expressed them. Where applicable I have translated these into Pin Yin but in any case each is described comprehensively in (I hope) clear English. The Pin Yin are of course the more useful terms for use within the international feng shui community.

# Acknowledgements

**This book is dedicated to my wife Sheila, without whom little of it would ever have seen the light of day, and to my children, Jaime, Alex, Thom, Jessie, Hen and Joey, who inspire me every day of my life.**

**This is to acknowledge my various teachers, some I have spent considerable time with, some just a few days, some I've never met face-to-face:**

Dr. Chuck Spezzano
Lency Spezzano
Derek Walters
Grand Master Chan Kun Wah
Grand Master Mas Kehardthum
Grand Master Tan Khoon Yong
Grand Master Raymond Lo
Master Howard Choy
Dr. Michael Paton
Professor Wang Yude
Dr/Grand Master Stephen Skinner
Si Fu Peter Leung
Peter Firebrace
Dato Joey Yap
Lillian Too
Jo Ching
Calvin Yap
Francis Leyau
Kwok Man Ho
Joe Karbo
Joe Gandolfo

Ken Wilber
Andrew Harvey
Karen Armstrong

**I owe a great debt also to the following**:

Kurt Rowe, without whose care, attention and skill above and beyond the call of duty, this book would never have made it into paper.

My friend the late High Heeled Healer, Anne-Marie Woodall – the world is a poorer place without you.

The late Dawn Gibbins – still and always an inspiration.

The late Jon Sandifer, ever the reasonable face of Feng Shui practice.

Lorna Bevan for the great gift both of Substack and her remarkable insights available there.

**Special Mentions:**

Jonni Javier – for my tv career, such as it has been.

Carlo Amadeo Reyneri di Lagnasco for the magnificent photo of the Taoist enclave at the top of Wudan Shang, unintentionally uncredited for the cover of *The Feng Shui Diaries.*

**Cover by:** the unique Ellie Spinelli
**San Sats & Cycles**: Nancy Canestaro

# Introduction

When I was first introduced to Ba Zi by Grandmaster Chan Kun Wah, I realised that I had stumbled upon something unique and extraordinary. If we define "healing" as forming a spectrum from performance enhancement at one extreme and actual physical change at the other, here was the most powerful tool I had ever encountered. After decades of attending to a variety of (mostly) Western teachers, gurus and facilitators, each of whom was to a greater or lesser extent re-inventing the wheel, here was the motherlode. My subsequent studies with Derek Walters, Joey Yap, Peter Leung, Mas Kehardthum, Howard Choy and the material of many others only served to confirm this initial conclusion. Ba Zi boasts more than two millennia of research and development and rules (some fixed and some flexible) that had been shown to work for all of that time. It was like a coming home.

This short book, along with a little effort and a Chinese Calendar, will teach you how to draft a Ba Zi and furnish you with all you need in order to interpret. That's where the real work starts of course. Mastery follows constant practice. This book alone will not take you to that destination, but it may show you the track that leads there.

What it will certainly do if you read it carefully is familiarise you with the Stems and Branches, the components that go to make up the Four Pillars of a Ba Zi, their functions and powers. You may (like me), be startled at how careful drafting can reveal a character, strengths and weaknesses as well as likely pitfalls and opportunities. You may find you develop your own relationships with these ancient archetypes. I hope so.

For further study, my book *The Feng Shui Diaries* includes many stories of Ba Zi in action and some good jokes. My courses online and in-person take this process a good deal further and as you might expect, come with a reading list and much additional material that either does not translate easily into the written word or will not squeeze into this modest volume.

One final note: many volumes of Chinese Metaphysics contain deliberate errors. Any errors in this little book are simply mistakes. Mine.

**Richard Ashworth***
**richardashworthfengshui@gmail.com**
**www.imperialfengshui.info**
**FaceBook: Richard Ashworth Feng Shui**
**Twitter: @FengShuiDiaries**
**Instagram: Richardashworthfengshui**

**A Note About Spirituality**: There is nothing inherently spiritual in Classical feng shui. Indeed of the many Chinese Masters I have known, very few have much of a handle on spirituality. I am prepared, however, to stick my neck out and state that pretty much any discipline is enhanced by spiritual awareness. This is probably more true of Ba Zi than most practices and although fixed rules apply to the Five Elements and the notions of Yin and Yang, the Tao which underlies everything does not appear to be subject to any such rules. So let me clarify that although above I dismiss many teachers in the world of woo-woo, I make a specific exception of Dr Chuck Spezzano's Psychology of Vision which underpins everything I do. If spirituality is terra incognita to you, you could usefully start there.

* Linked In: Richard Ashworth Blue Sky

# Origins: Animals, Elements, Time and Place

Broadly, authentic Chinese feng shui has come to us down two distinct lines of descent. One of these has brought us the ideas of Yin and Yang and the Book of Changes; the other the Five Elements (or Wu Xing) and the Animals of the Chinese Zodiac. Both appear to have their origins in shamanic practices dating back at least four thousand years.

The first line of descent is from the diviners of the Shang Dynasty (1600–1046 BCE) who found that when they baked the shells of river turtles (which they rendered extinct in the process) patterns of lines appeared. Over time they noticed that when employed in divinatory procedures, a broken (or yin) line appeared to offer a reliable "No" in answer to a question and an unbroken one a reliable "Yes". Over time they and their successors during the Zhou Dynasty (1046–256 BCE) learned to consult clusters of two and then three lines – from which are derived the Trigrams – and finally the sixty-four six-line figures or Hexagrams of the *Book of Changes,* I Ching or Yi.

This may be the moment to point out that for the early diviners life must have been nasty, brutish and short. The job of the diviner was to ensure that their family, tribe or nation was safe, sheltered and nourished in a world which was largely not yet understood. From which we can draw the conclusion that feng shui, BaZi and associated practices would not have survived to the present day if they did not work. Put simply feng shui and Ba Zi must have made for prosperity.

It is, however, the other line of descent that concerns us here: over millennia a series of Chinese observers had meanwhile noticed that the progress of the seasons of the year mirrored the hours of the day. There was a spring to the day if you will and a dawn to the year; a winter in the cold of the night and a midnight around the Winter Solstice. It was clear that early in the day, dawn breaks and things start to move and equally that the year begins in a similar way with the return of warmth and light. They called this first phase whether relating to the first few months of the year or the hours around dawn, the Element *Wood*.

*Phase* is actually a much more accurate term than Element. These qualities Wood, Fire, Earth, Metal and Water belong to successive locations on the compass as well as on the calendar and clock face.

Wood broadly means constant movement. What plants and trees do which human beings, snails, rocks, ingots, buildings and digestive biscuits do not, is move constantly. This is Wood. Which means that the desk you may be sitting at or the chair you are on, is not really Wood at all. Of course it's different from rock or steel but to many Masters it's actually Earth. Wood is alive and we can tell that because it is in constant movement, just as we know as a general rule that a plant is alive because it is growing.

These observers noted two varieties of Wood: yin and yang, that is when qi (often equated to energy but ambience or feeling might serve us better for now) is respectively moving gently and thoroughly, or when it is moving suddenly and rapidly. In time to the Yang Wood phase was given the name Tiger whose hours are between 3 and 5 a.m. and whose month is February; Yin was named Rabbit (East/5–7a.m./March). Further observation showed that the Tiger and Rabbit Double Hours coincided with the sun moving from the North East through the East, that is to say with the dawn. In other words they were dealing with phases both of time and space. Which incidentally means that learning Ba Zi amounts to learning a great deal of Classical feng shui theory at the same time. Perhaps 40% of authentic feng shui amounts to Ba Zi on the ground.

Observers noticed also that though the dawn often rose rapidly with the Tiger – the closer you are to the equator the more true this is – a relatively gentle phase of less urgent movement followed. Thus we have at first Yang Wood which is urgent, immediate and unsubtle, followed by Yin Wood which is in the words of the *Book of Changes*, "gentle and thorough but ultimately adamant".

And here we see how Yin contrasts with Yang: a tree is reckoned Yang Wood; although it will bend it is hard to break, but to eliminate a tree all you need is a chain saw: that is to say Yang Metal which is equally unsubtle. Yin Wood on the other hand is more like grass, it will take root wherever there is light and moisture (that is Fire and Water) and of course Earth* but if you try to get rid of it with a chainsaw, all you get is muddy. This is Yin and Yang.

It was actually Buddhist monks in historical times who gave the phases their names: Tiger, Rabbit and Dragon, respectively Yang Wood, Yin Wood and Yang Earth-in-Wood. The qualities of the Tiger include fine eyesight, patience and speed; of the Rabbit, sensitivity, conscience and attention. Dragons express Yang Earth-in-Wood by being able to transform themselves and others. The Dragon (South East/7–9a.m./April) can wiggle their nose and change things just as the high pressure of the thunderstorm precedes the relief of April showers. The Dragon is the magician of the Chinese Zodiac.

In feng shui practice we might say that Wood gets things done: in order to do so, we get up early, locate East, ensure we are in decent light, colour things green and get started. And of course because the only constant is change, sometimes that's not a good idea.

The next phase is *Fire*: things speed up and heat up, towards both the middle of the day and the middle of the year. The Fire time is from 9 a.m. to 3 p.m., the months May to July. The

---

* What about Metal? As Metal can destroy Wood, you might consider it the necessary aspect of mortality. Every phase ends. Some would say that diversity emerges at the price of mortality.

corresponding Animals are Snake (Yin Fire) Horse (Yang Fire) and Sheep (Yin Earth-in Fire).

You may have noticed already that the sequence of the Stems (that is the Animals) is not quite the traditional cycle of production (Wood, Fire, Earth, Metal, Water) but a variation which also puts Earth in the middle albeit in a different way: Wood, Wood, Earth; Fire, Fire, Earth and so on. In both sequences Earth is best thought of as the reference point, the ground upon which we stand. Unlike the other Elements the direction of motion of Earth is no motion at all. Earth such as mountains and boulders is of course resistant to movement.

The Snake then occupies the hours between 9 and 11 a.m. and the month of May (though all of these Chinese Solar Months begin slightly later than their Western counterparts). The Snake lives South East and is Yin Fire, sometimes called Candle Flame, more about light than heat. Her lifelong issue for better or for worse is the shedding of light upon things, often this amounts to the pursuit of truth, sometimes its opposite.

And as we shall discover, many of these remarks can be applied to the events of the corresponding year and to those who were born in them. Someone born in the Year of the Horse will enjoy some of the features of the Horse such as passion and haste. As we shall discover even later, with changes of nuance a similar principle applies to our Month, Hour and Day of Birth.

The Horse (due South/the double hour around noon/June) is reckoned Yang Fire and Horses are often seekers of attention, Yang Fire mimics the upwards movements of the rainforest canopy in search of the warmth of the sun. The final Branch (that is Animal) of Fire is the Sheep, seeking home and company as the sun passes its zenith.

Naturally if we seek attention we seek Fire, the South, illumination, the colour red and upwards movement. And naturally because nature does not generally work in straight lines, sometimes we shouldn't.

Which brings us to the *Metal* of late afternoon and early evening. Metal stands for precision. Precision is the mother of contention: so the Yang Metal Monkey (South West/3–5 p.m./August) as you might expect is a Branch of rebellion. As is the Rooster (due West/5–7 p.m./September) though Rooster rebellions tend to be more clandestine (like the French Revolution of 1789) than the straightforward outrage of Monkey Revolutions (like the US Declaration of Independence in 1776). The positive side of Metal of course is that it is the Element of technology as well as glamour, both in their different ways representing proportion and precision. Metal's motion is circular, generally centrifugal but sometimes centripetal.

The Earth-in-Metal of the Dog, a totem of faith and consistency (or obstinacy if you prefer to see it that way round) occupies October, part of the North West and the hours between 7 and 9 p.m. Just as schools and banks close late afternoon and consider the lessons of the day, so in the autumn we assess the harvest and prepare for winter.

The Pig next in sequence, occupies the latter part of the North West as the day starts to close and the November nights draw in between 9 and 11 p.m. Water is communication and the Pig is Yin, one meaning of which is small. Water also connotes emotion, so as you might expect, the multi-talented Pig is not generally effusive. All Water is in search of all other Water. Water's direction of travel is down; as long as there is an incline, Water will follow it.

The Rat (North/December/around midnight) is the counterpoint. Rat years are Yang Water. They feature encounters with Water like 1972, the year of Watergate and 1912 when the Titanic went down. And you'll recall Watergate pivoted on Richard Nixon's verbal incontinence: it was a stream of words which he would later wish to deny but that were recorded for posterity, that did for him.

Finally the Ox (January/1–3 a.m./North East) is Yin Earth-in-Water, representing the sleepy time that accompanies the year's end as well as what some call the witching hour. Oxen are proverbially sensitive but also hard to move. Oxen, you might recall, often wear blinkers.

So that's the Animals or Branches. When they are modified by a *Stem* they become *Pillars,* (which when placed one atop the other is what they look like). So the Stem Yin Water above the Branch Rabbit gives us the Water Rabbit Pillar of 2023 thus:

癸 (Yin) Water
卯 Rabbit

And so on.

**A Note About the Credentials of the Ba Zi:** the Gan Zi Cycle of sixty Pillars unites two early measurements of time: the Heavenly Stems and Earthly Branches (or Animals).

**The Stems** derive from an early Chinese system of 10-day weeks. It seems that this was based upon observation of the rising and setting of the five visible planets: Jupiter, Mars, Saturn, Venus and Mercury: Jupiter appears as a greeny brown; Mars is proverbially the Red Planet; Saturn is a brown colour, Venus white and Mercury a dark spot against the sun. They rise in that order which reflects and may have been the inspiration for the familiar Cycle of Production which of course runs Wood, Fire, Earth, Metal, Water and so on (not quite like the sequence of the Branches where Earth is central in a different way). This sequence of planets and corresponding gods and goddesses appears in many cultures worldwide including in the names of our own Western days of the week.

Probably for reasons similar to the Chinese, many cultures start with a 10-day week. 10 is a handy number for managing (approximately) 30-day lunar months. But many progress to a 7-day week which continues to respect the same planets and deities but unlike the Chinese system takes no note of rising or setting, that is yin and yang. 4 weeks of 7 days again approximates to a lunar month – which is actually around 29 days of course – making an equally workable system.

**The origins of the Branches** in observation of the equivalence between the phases of energy during day and year, we explore above but there are two conclusions (at least) to draw:

1. The Gan Zi Cycle of sixty Stems and branches represents something real and physical, a measuring of time that is unlike our own calendar, not based upon arbitrary choices months of 30, 31 or 29 days but on the behaviour of actual planets.
2. The word "approximate" is an important one. There are Chinese Masters who consider feng shui (and hence Ba Zi) to be an exact science. There are also many who notice how much approximation is involved. In the introduction to his famous *Yi*, the late Wu Jing Nuan emphasises this. The Elements and Yin and Yang may perhaps be bound by rules but the Tao does not appear to be. As an illustration, perhaps consider the astonishing fact that there is such a thing possible as a solar eclipse: a relatively close body, diameter about the width of the continental US, appears almost exactly the same size as one that is vast and 93 million miles away and can from time to time block its light. It's a sobering thought that it won't be so in a billion years, as the moon moves further away.

Consider also that there are 29ish days in a lunar month and 365¼ days in a Solar year. If the moon would travel just a little slower and the Earth a little faster, there would be precisely 12 lunar months in a calendar year. But there aren't. We must be as precise as we can but it is only appropriately humble to be aware that absolute precision is impossible.

In the spirit of Taoist thought I invite you to draw no conclusions from the above.

<u>A Note About the Implications of Each Pillar:</u> Time moves from the right to the left of a Ba Zi: from the Year Pillar via the Month and Day to the Hour.

**To be born in the Year of, say, the Sheep is** to have family tradition, deep history, DNA, family parents and grandparents represented by the Sheep. The Year Pillar being the first to receive the qi, does a great deal of heavy lifting. You can tell a great deal about someone from the Year Pillar alone. The Year represents our earliest and most formative years, and the environment into which we were born. It's perfectly reasonable as some do to draw a variety of conclusions from the Year Pillar alone.

**If instead that Sheep falls in the Month Pillar** it will tend to represent education, peers, siblings, exes and the work environment. Shallower history perhaps.

**The Day Pillar** stands more particularly for you yourself and your most intimate relationships. The Day Branch is reckoned among other things to be your true partner.

**Your Hour Pillar** stands for your dreams, your children, and those deep wishes that you may never share. Your **Life House** which we'll deal with elsewhere stands for what calls to you.

Here are the Four Pillars for this moment, as I write:

| Hour | Day | Month | Year |
|---|---|---|---|
| Fire | Fire | Metal | Water |
| 丙 | 丁 | 辛 | 癸 |
| Horse | Sheep | Rooster | Rabbit |
| 午 | 未 | 酉 | 卯 |

For purposes of interpretation a feng shui Master will be as interested in your Day as your Year Pillar as it, and particularly the Day Stem, represents who you really are.

Observing time passing from Year to Month and so on can make certain processes clear: the structure of the Year Pillar – how Stem and Branch interact – may be duplicated or contradicted by the Month and Day Pillars but for better or worse the relationship between these Pillars tells us a lot about the learning process over time, especially in regard to intimate relationship. A Day Pillar that is very different to the Year Pillar speaks of markedly different decisions from the parental example.

You may find these comments helpful as you read about the Animals especially if you're examining your own Ba Zi at the same time.

**A Note About Tze**: The character Tze connoting Rat carries a range of further meanings. Among them are "baby" and "teacher". The philosophers Lao Tze and Kung Fu Tze as well as Zhuang Tze, Mo Tze and indeed Sun Tze don't share a surname but an epithet which indicates respect and learning. It means something like "professor" in this context. The Anglo-Saxon historian Bede was referred to as the "Venerable" which is pretty close.

# Meet the Animals of the Chinese Zodiac

For more on the Animals go to https://bit.ly/2NAB3Lu where you will also usually find forecasts for the year, (Animal by Animal).

### The Rat

**Who Is a Rat?**

**Years:** 1948, 1960, 1972, 1984, 1996, 2008, 2020, 2032.

**Month*:** December.

**Hour:** 23.00–01.00

**Day:** You'll need a Chinese Calendar or an expert for this.

**What Is a Rat?**

The Rat is Yang Water but with a hidden stem of Yin Water, that is to say *pure* Water, the only Chinese Animal that is so pure. All Water on this planet, unless interfered with by outside forces, is connected with and on the same level as all other Water. Sea level at Zeebrugge is the same as sea level at Miami. If I spill my cup of tea here in Surrey and you spill yours in Taiwan, sooner or later they'll mix. It may take aeons but they'll mix. This powerful idea may clarify the connection between Water and communication. Water of course always goes downwards and cannot be compressed.

Someone said that we have two ears and one mouth for a good reason: that we should listen twice as much as we speak. The issues relating to Water are listening and speaking while keeping the ratios right. The Rat can easily miss this. Some of us are elected primarily to talk and the Yang Water of the Rat makes them the talker of the Chinese Zodiac. An unbalanced or

* Caution: the start of the Chinese month can be as early as the 4th and as late as the 9th.

distressed Rat tends to either clam up or run off at the mouth. Awareness of the need to listen can be a lesson but the Rat on the Beam tuning in to the idle chatter amid the port fumes and cigar smoke is one of Rat's roles.*

I've written elsewhere about the Rats in the House of Windsor. Interestingly both Prince Harry and his father, King Charles, are Rats. Charles's career has been one of juggling his often outspoken opinions with the privilege of his position. Harry's lessons may be similar, making observation of his father's conundrum invaluable. Rats can blurt or be schtum.

The Rat is supreme in the realm of ideas, a planner, a plotter and a deep thinker. He thinks ahead, sometimes to the detriment of his awareness of the present. This makes him a good chess player but not so great at poker. He is apt to be too controlling for games that require openness – even to good fortune. That sort of uncertainty can be painful. Your average Rat wants the credit and to get that he has to be in control.

In conversation you may find that the mature Rat second guesses in a very distinctive way: typically he gets his correspondent to commit to a position before he states his; a very useful quality in a teacher but not everyone's cup of tea in a collaborator. The Dragon and the Monkey, even the Ox, may find this reassuring but it drives the Horse and the Tiger wild and to some extent even the passive Dog.

Being big talkers and travellers, Rats are traditionally suited to work involving communication: sales, oratory and persuasion. In the collaboration with the Rabbit, Rooster and Horse that my teacher, Derek Walters, (himself a Rat) called the *Flowers of Love*, the Rat is the talker, the chatter-up if you will, where the Rooster provides the glamour, the Horse the passion and the Rabbit a warm welcome. A Rat with the assistance of

* In particular the Metal Rat of 1960.

these other Animals is effortlessly successful and charismatic; to find them all in one Ba Zi speaks of a remarkably magnetic individual. If that person's Ba Zi – tantalisingly – has three of them, whichever may be missing indicates his weaknesses. None of the other Flowers though is ever much at ease alone in the company of the Rat.

An unbalanced Rat talks too much and listens selectively. A balanced one gets it exactly right; he is a fascinating talker and a skilled listener. But willful deafness can be a point of pride. Blessed with an orderly mind and excellent retention, a Rat can consider his own ignorance of a subject a reflection upon the subject rather than upon himself. This sort of Rat needs to learn to value the convictions of others, especially if they are derived from premises he does not accept.

The Rat is a guardian, a watcher. Sometimes he is self-appointed and the unbalanced Rat has a particular blindness that leads him to believe that his opinion is an absolute. This is more accentuated and less well-informed in his partnership with the Ox in what some call the House of Creativity.

Despite the discrepancy in their apparent power, the Ox has the upper hand in their special relationship with the Rat; they are technically Secret Friends, that is mutual *amulets.** The Ox can be a particularly obdurate and dominating learner, sometimes drawing conclusions to which he is not entitled and sticking like a limpet to any conclusion he can justify. In these circumstances the Ox is not so much partner or indeed student of the Rat as tormentor. Perhaps surprisingly when Ox and Rat are together it is the Ox who calls the tunes. That the Ox

* Feng Shui Masters may recommend a protective amulet for each year as it arises. If you visit Chinatown in say Singapore in January of a Rat year, you will find the stalls well stocked with little jade Rat amulets which they know tourists will snap up in the belief that this is the correct charm for the year. They will also have plenty of Ox amulets for the cannier Chinese who know the rules.

rules the Rat and thus sets the agenda in Ox and Rat years is an important consideration. See comments below about Metal Ox Barack Obama in the Rat and Ox Years 2008 and 2009.

A very conscious Rat can make good use of his blindness to the value of other people's positions. She is likely to be able to explain things that baffle others and to derive laws from this gift. To have no explanation, however, is to open herself up to chaos. If she knows this about herself she can master even the most abstract discipline.

The Rat is versatile and multi-talented though not as notably so as the Pig of whom he is often jealous or the Dragon who can baffle him despite their mutual affinity. Rat's Yang Water can speak of profligacy with money. So the typical Rat is a brilliant small businessman but often a poor tycoon.

In the power triad with the Dragon and Monkey, the Rat may appear to overvalue the hands-on deftness of the Monkey because he finds the Monkey easier to control and may envy the Dragon his magic. Twin Rats Robert Plant and John Bonham and Monkey Jimmy Page of Led Zeppelin (formed in the Monkey Year of 1968) may be a good example of this creative tension.

And it is this potential for envy that is the other big weakness of the Rat. He can't admire what he can't himself master. This can lead to him not getting credit for originality of mind. Consider Water Rat Alan Turing of Enigma fame.

The Rat is subject to the so-called *Ingratitude Penalty.* This means broadly that a Rabbit child may resent the upbringing the Rat parent gave them. In response the parent may consider the child ungrateful. Obviously enough it's endemic in Rat and Rabbit Years and among those who have Rat and/or Rabbit in their Four Pillars. But since these things are metaphors (not *just* metaphors, everything is a metaphor on some level) it can show up as Parent/Child, Employer/Employee and of course, as above, as King/Prince.

Technically this is Yang Water overwhelming Yin Wood and a cursory inspection of the events of 2023 would indicate that not only were King Charles's sons something of a headache to him but there was more industrial unrest both sides of the Atlantic than in any year perhaps since the previous Rabbit of 2011. And if you stretched the dynamic to Empire/Colony it offers insight into the rash of Commonwealth countries seeking republic status and indeed Russia's incursions into the sovereign territory of Ukraine which it sometimes characterises as an ungrateful offspring.

Diametrically opposed to the Rat on compass, clock and calendar is the Horse. This, the relationship between Water and Fire is often misunderstood: a great deal of Water will indeed quench Fire but a little will provoke it. Think of the way Water may be used against a massive industrial blaze: just a little will add oxygen to the flames as the Water evaporates, it will take significantly more to put it out altogether. So if we think of Fire as inspiration, Water may be thought of as discussion or criticism. Most ideas gain from the air of discussion but too much especially when comment is critical, can suppress creativity. The impact of what is technically a *Clash* can vary between stimulation and destruction.

The Sheep is technically a *Harm* to the Rat. This is because the Rat's Secret Friend the Ox is opposed to the Sheep. When Sheep and Rat coincide they may fall out over issues that actually concern the Ox rather than themselves.

Similarly, the Rooster brings the Rat *Breakup*. This can be quite literal. In a Rooster Year the Rat may feel that the Rooster's Yin Metal is not quite enough to fuel his Yang Water. In a marriage this can mean spouses' interests and priorities move in different directions. Watch the House of Windsor closely for this one.

The Rat can be a fickle partner but an attentive parent, albeit one who may have favourites. The awakened Rat is absolutely even-handed; that in itself is quite a gift.

## The Ox

**Who Is an Ox?**

**Years:** 1949, 1961, 1973, 1985, 1997, 2009.
**Month***: January
**Hour:** 01.00–03.00
**Day:** You'll need a Chinese Calendar or an expert for this.

**What Is an Ox?**

The distinctive quality of the Ox is insistence, not persistence so much because the Ox's Yin Earth makes for minor blockage, more a blackout curtain than a rampart. The Ox is, in many ways, the most sensitive Zodiac Animal. This is often expressed in what looks like obstinacy but is better understood as puzzlement at being disagreed with. In discourse you may find that an Ox has firm principles that on examination are more like prejudices or assumptions. They are often nonetheless firm as well as correct for all that. As a rule, don't expect flexibility of mind from an Ox; they know what they know and are often not keen to venture beyond. The Ox may wear blinkers. Never forget, however, how sensitive they are.

The key quality of the Ox is fertility, for better or worse. In a Ba Zi that may indicate fecundity or the reverse but it will usually be an issue. The *Hidden Stems* within a Ba Zi (which we will discuss in due course) and the Metal that Earth produces may clarify this.

The Ox's gifts are very often practical rather than intellectual. The intellectually gifted Ox is extraordinarily powerful. Because of her position between the Rat and the Tiger, the Ox can sometimes vacillate from a feline ferocity – that does not really suit her – to a Rat-like charm that she may not be able to sustain.

---

* Caution: the start of the Chinese month can be as early as the 4th and as late as the 9th.

Watch out for the Ox who you seem on first acquaintance to have known all your life but who then becomes uncontactable. In certain contexts this is called "ghosting".

With her allies the Snake and the Rooster, she forms a team which is of the Metal element. That is to say that the alliance is likely to be analytical, linear, judgemental and competitive. Where the ground rules are clear, this is an unstoppable combination. Not when they're not. But these three make a great legal team with the Rooster charming the jury, the Snake exposing truth as they do and the Ox sticking to the point. When the rules are unclear, however, the Metal alliance can falter. Then the Ox can become judgemental in a more covert sort of way, being less liable to argue than to judge silently. Without the Snake and the Rooster, the Ox is more barrack room lawyer than barrister.

Working in such a team, the Metal qualities of logic, reason and competition, are less important than consistency. In dealing with the Ox, it is important to remember not only that she is partly Metal but also that she may deny this fact even to herself.

The hour of the Ox (1–3.00 a.m.) is when the worlds of spirit and flesh are closest. She has a deep spiritual agenda and may be attracted to organised religion, where the Ox appears in the Ba Zi may indicate when this attraction is strongest. The gifts of mediumship and divination are essentially Ox gifts.

**A Note About Hand Drafting:** There are hundreds of apps and links which will calculate a Ba Zi for you in seconds. Can I suggest that speed is not necessarily the point? In drafting a Ba Zi we are concerned both with outcome and process. You will need to learn to read from a Chinese calendar in order to draft by hand. It's not rocket science but it'll take you a little while, I expect. That time need not be wasted. Nor need it be fruitless.

There is no direct relationship between effort and results, nor indeed between time taken and satisfactory outcome. Meanwhile the universe is talking to us all the time. It may be in the form of a feather falling at our feet, a snatch of conversation or a tune at the edge of our hearing. When I am drawing up a Ba Zi, I aim to take note of such things and also of my own feelings and pre-occupations. We and all things are connected, so it may be that I am being told about the subject of the Ba Zi.

And of course, I aim to be receptive. This may involve downing tools altogether and feeling into myself for a while. The state I want to be in is one of benevolent openness. Never forget that you are in service to your client.

The apt student, by the way, can draft what matters as quickly as an app.

Oxen may nonetheless be attached to ancestral dogma. Fundamentalism of all sorts – political and social as well as religious – is a common trait. Ox is not always good at questioning tradition or second-hand wisdom that has come down on good authority. So she will often quote great men not because their words are wise but because they are great. Bob Dylan's advice "Don't follow leaders and watch your parking meters" goes over the head of the immature Ox but is the credo of the life-wisened one.

With the Dragon, Dog and Sheep, the Ox forms the Literary Alliance. Some call this confluence the Four Earths and think of it as negative. The fact is that it is a demanding combination. If the Dragon is missing from it, for instance, many think of this alliance as poisonous but an assembly of the vehicles of expression without anything new to say is probably more like it.

This coincidence of the three Earth Branches Ox, Sheep and Dog in time or space, known as the *Bullying Curse*, is a challenge to a strong Ba Zi and can be the ruin of a weak one. As it consists of Dog, Sheep and Ox, expect it to occur in January, July and October of any Earth year like 2024 or 2027. If you spot these three in the Year, Month and Day (in any order) of a Ba Zi you can be pretty certain this is someone who was marginalized early. Look for playground bullying and that kind of thing.

Barack Obama may be the world's most famous Ox though he actually has a Sheep in his month pillar. This makes for a home-loving and secure man. This is heightened by his day stem (the character that rules the day he was born) which has an unusual affinity both with the Ox and the Sheep. This like so many Oxen, is a man who loves his babies.

Obama may also illustrate the cyclical power of the Ox. The Ox rules the Rat and hence the Rat Year and during the Rat Year of 2008 and his subsequent first year in office, Obama could do no wrong. But once that Ox Year of 2009 was gone, he could get very little done.

The Ox has a love-hate (or *Harm*) relationship with the irritatingly spontaneous and extrovert Horse to whom she cannot help nonetheless being drawn. Nor is she that keen on the Rabbit who can help herself to the Ox's fresh vegetables or the Tiger who somehow often manages to exploit her.

Technically, Ox and Dragon form a *Breakup*. Ox/Dragon marriages take a great deal of mutual understanding. The Ox is naturally restrictive, the Dragon knows no boundaries. As you might expect, Ox and Dragon together in a Ba Zi can be quite confusing.

Central point: the Ox's power is cyclical, arriving every twelve years and lasting for two. Don't waste it!

**A Note About Oxen and Rats**: The Ox is notable for sticking to things beyond their sell-by date as well as periodically dominating the Rat. Within an individual's Ba Zi it also often connotes a spiritual or religious path as does the Sheep. As a Year Pillar it may suggest birth into a religious or spiritual tradition; in the Month or Day a conversion; in the Hour, children with such convictions. Oxen know how to pray.

## The Tiger

### Who Is a Tiger?

**Years:** 1950, 1962, 1974, 1986, 1998, 2010.
**Month*:** February
**Hour:** 03.00–05.00
**Day:** You'll need a Chinese Calendar or an expert for this.

### What Is a Tiger?

Because the Tiger is generally considered Yang Wood but actually consists of three different elements, he is an especially versatile predator. There is nothing wrong with being a predator of course, except that it can imply a very rigid view of the world. Tigers often don't play well with others, not because their egos are in the way (unlike the Dragon, the Pig, the Rooster or the Horse) but because for them, work and play are very distinct activities. They can up to a point frolic with other Tigers but every alliance tends to focus on an outcome. It's no coincidence that 1974 Tiger Victoria Beckham is the Spice Girl who moved on.

The Tiger never forgets. For the unbalanced Tiger no slight, insult or rejection can be allowed to go unredressed. He may wait a lifetime but he will get his revenge. Earth Tiger Joseph Stalin typified this as Leon Trotsky was able to confirm the hard way. On the other hand the balanced Tiger will always repay a debt and will go out of his way to acknowledge assistance. The Tiger marks your card early.

The typical qualities of Yang Wood are sharp eyes, a strong will and swift movement. The Tiger stalks his prey silently and pounces when he is ready. He can wait days as long as he is not hungry. A needy Tiger is very dangerous. Never scorn the Tiger. The Tiger will not forget.

---

* Caution: the start of the Chinese Month of the Tiger falls on the 4th or 5th, depending on the year.

Being Yang Wood which is about movement, the Tiger needs elbow room. Each Element contains a particular form of aggression if you will. For the Tiger it's space. Always give the Tiger plenty of leeway. Russia of course is to the North East of Europe which may shed light upon the notorious Russian need to expand to the West and South as demonstrated in the Tiger Year of 2022. Equally in the Wood Tiger year of 1914 more young men set out to kill more young men than at any other time in history. 1938, the Year of *lebensraum*, was also a Tiger.

The Tiger will often have a fresh view of things which makes him the eyes of the team he makes up with the Horse and the Dog. The Horse is front of house, the Dog the keeper of records and the Tiger the hit man.

In terms of human relations, the Tiger may be the most Yang of the animals; that is swift, sharp and unsubtle. The Earth Hidden Stem (more on the sequence of Hidden Stems underlying the Stems themselves elsewhere) he inherits from his predecessor in the Zodiac the Ox, is turned miraculously from Yin to Yang when he receives it. The unbalanced Tiger knows no mercy and expects none. And in this he has altered the dogma he receives from the Ox – do as you would be done by – into a personal code. This alteration can amount to perversion and make for serious misunderstandings; the unconscious Tiger probably knows himself less well than any other animal. His ruthlessness which he can wear as a badge of honour, is often simply a failure to open up to interdependence with others.

This reluctance may clarify how Tiger and Pig behave as *Secret Friends*. The Pig is no threat to the Tiger and so may make a perfect confidante. Tiger/Pig marriages can work both ways round: Water and Wood can be mutually supportive: the Tiger may be fuelled by the Pig and the Pig drawn out in return. Note, however, that these two also form a *Breakup* when the divisive issue may be a mistrust of interdependence.

Of all descriptions "dependent" is the most insulting to the Tiger. They *will* not depend. This makes relationship an act of will. With a true act of will, the Tiger forms the most enduring relationships. If it is not truly a choice but a resigned agreement to bend himself out of shape, all around him will distort also. Sometimes the truly unconscious Tiger thinks this reflects a merciless world in which he has been clever in getting his revenge in first. This logic doesn't work and the smarter Tiger knows this.

But even the smartest Tiger is not in the clear because the corollary of foregoing revenge appears to be falling on her sword. This is a mistake too. Most of us prefer not to live by the law of the jungle but then most of us are not as well-equipped for it.

Metal is generally considered to represent logical thought, authority and competition. The Tiger is elementally the opposite of Metal; the wooden Tiger likes to think of himself as logical, but instinctive (or even automatic) is a better description. Generally he can only make use of Metal early on in life or at the inception of a process. After that he can deceive himself that he knows what to do and that he is beyond advice. His chief adversaries are the (Yang Metal) Monkey whose frivolity he can't stand and the Snake who won't offer him a static target. Note as ever that the other Pillars in a Ba Zi can temper or accentuate this.

The really unbalanced Tiger (Yang Wood day stem for instance born in February) considers himself bold and resolute but truly is hanging onto past (mother) stuff that ought to have been completed. The admission of this might affront his pride and he is unlikely to do it.

Richard Bandler (himself a notoriously ruthless 1950 Tiger) the Godfather of Neuro-Linguistic Programming, used to say that the person with the most flexible behaviour has control. The Tiger is the yangest woodenest of the animals. He is so flexible that he can be completely immovable as things change around him. Discomfort is not an issue to many Tigers. In a sales situation – paired with the Rabbit in the so-called House of Progress# – the Rabbit opens the sale with sheer charm but the Tiger closes it.

This can be his role in the alliance with the Monkey, Pig and Snake sometimes called the Four Terminals#: the Monkey sells the traveller a ticket, the Pig may offer to accompany him, and the Snake can enchant with tales of exotic locations, but the Tiger makes sure they pay in full. Without the Tiger in the Ba Zi this combination can lack edge, implying restricted movement as well as cash-flow issues.

And of course (because they are all technically *Stations*) any conjunction of these four has implications for travel and movement, Watch for the Tiger Day in the Monkey month – proverbially a day of short tempers and specifically road rage. Equally, watch for the Fire Penalty – frustration due to interference – whenever Tiger and Monkey coincide with Snake; ubiquitous of course in Tiger Years like 2022, Snake Years like 2025 and Monkeys such as 2028.

A tender parent and an implacable father-in-law, a good leader but an erratic motivator, at his worst, the keynote of the Tiger is an uneasy combination between a long memory and a short fuse. At his best he is the sort of leader you would gladly die for. At worst she'll do the job for you.

**A Note About Tigers, Monkeys and Ghosts**: Every Element has its own peculiar form of aggression, that is to say, will to live. For Wood it is space, for Metal something like accuracy. This can mean that in their Yang form Tigers can demand legroom to which they are not entitled and the Monkey can be self-righteous. In the extreme, the Tiger will clear all from his path and a Monkey believe that he is infallible. The Monkey of Chinese legend is said to have leapt to the moon to erase his misdeeds from the Akashic Record.

The Monkey Month apart, being also the time of summer vacations, features the Festival of the Hungry Ghosts, that is of those dead or alive whose appetites are impossible to satisfy.

Monkey and Tiger are of course extreme opposites: Metal against Wood, West against East, reason against intuition, science versus poetry and so on. So… on a Tiger Day in the Monkey Month it may be that the Tiger taking up three lanes in his Tesla on a hot August afternoon is on the same freeway as the Monkey driving as if he is immortal and infallible. On such a day it may be wise to stay off the roads.

## The Rabbit

**Who Is a Rabbit?**

**Years:** 1939, 1951, 1963, 1975, 1987, 1999.

**Month*:** March

**Hour:** 05.00–07.00

**Day:** You'll need a Chinese Calendar.

**What Is a Rabbit?**

The Rabbit is Yin Wood, essentially gentle and domestic. Her time is early morning; the legend has it that she and the Rooster swapped places which is why the Zodiac Rooster crows not at dawn but at dusk. The Rabbit rules the spring therefore – think of March Hares and Easter Bunnies – and the Rooster the autumn. This story may also serve to illustrate the mistrust that can exist between Rabbit and the Yin Metal Rooster who are opposites in all sorts of ways: East/West, Wood/Metal, Poetry/Science, Intuition/Measurement, Humility/Vanity and more.

The Rabbit is subtle, in keeping with her Yin nature. She provides service readily and is often suited to catering and caring. But her preparedness to roll up her sleeves makes her the unexpected queen of networking. If you want to be introduced to the person in charge, ask a Rabbit, however low down the food chain they appear to be.

Although giving an impression of reluctance to be in the spotlight, Rabbits are often performers but equally often are more at home behind the scenes. Writer-composer Tim Minchin fits this bill. Devoted dad David Beckham perhaps also and strangely introvert ex-Prime Minister Gordon Brown. All clearly pretty good at making connections also.

The Rabbit can wait her turn; vigilance and patience are typical. Her natural allies are the Pig and the Sheep. This

* Caution: Chinese months can start as early as the 4th and as late as the 9th.

is a house-proud team and the Rabbit is a team player. Her unexpected friend is the Dog who values her ability to charm without threat.

The Rabbit also belongs to the gathering known as the Flowers of Love*(or Plumflowers) along with the Horse, the Rooster and Rat. She may often find herself clearing up behind these three extroverts and quite often the cuddle-bunny will obtain a life partner from the leavings of her more blatantly glamorous colleagues.

Rabbit can easily fall out with the Horse. In a Horse Year the Rabbit may be overwhelmed by the demands (especially public ones) being made upon her, just as the Horse may find the Rabbit's support inconstant.

Rabbit tends to be conservative with a small "c". Early rising is typical but the yang of early alertness may be balanced by the yin of sleeping in. Lazybones or insomniac, sleeping is an issue. This is yin and yang.

In some ways the Rabbit epitomises Yin. Yang Wood may be characterised as assertive and dynamic, hard to remove like a tree. Yin Wood is more of an outward expansion like the spread of grass. What these two expressions of Wood have in common is irresistibility. But they are very different types of irresistibility. To counter Yang Wood we need Yang Metal: an axe will cut down the biggest tree. But you could attack a lawn with that same axe and not remove all the grass in a lifetime. This is the power of Yin Wood.

Wood is both stubborn and flexible. Yin Wood (as characterised by *Soen*, the wind of the South East) is irresistible

* #This term and several others I use are the brainchild of the man who first introduced me to the Chinese Zodiac, Derek Walters, still the only Western authority respected to any degree in Asia. I sometimes tell my students that of the many thousands of books written on Chinese Astrology in the West, 99% are either nonsense or derived from Derek's *The Complete Guide to Chinese Astrology*. Or both. Now in his late 80s, still worth following on Instagram.

as well as organised: "gentle and thorough but ultimately adamant" as the *Book of Changes* or *Yi* has it.

Hexagram 53 of the Yi (aka *I Ching*), "Gradual Progress" relates also: the tree on the mountain grows against all the odds either because it throws itself absolutely upon the mercy of the Tao or because it has a detailed plan that it follows meticulously. Or both.

The Rabbit is said to cause the Dragon (next in sequence) to lose money. Perhaps the Dragon is distracted by a neighbour so apparently different in nature. These two are not a great pairing but the unlikely fact is that the Rabbit sitting between the Tiger and the Dragon, shares qualities with both. Do not mistake the Rabbit for a victim.

Partnership with the Tiger is sometimes formalised as the House of Progress. The Rabbit offers carrot while the Tiger wields a stick. More may be achieved perhaps with a kind word and a gun than with a kind word alone.

Wood represents bone, spine and hair as well as eyes: the light is Fire but the receiving organ is Wood. The Rabbit is often not strong in these regards unlike the Tiger. This again, is yin and yang.

Finally, it's worth appreciating that the wooden table you're probably seated by is wood but not Wood. Wood is always growing which is not true of anything else; not animals, people, cutting edges or stones. Usable Wood in feng shui terms is alive. Many Masters consider dead Wood to be Earth, motionless and ashen.

**A Note About Rabbits and Cats**: In Vietnam this Zodiac Animal is called the Cat. Intuitively this does not sit right, the ideogram so clearly has long ears. Furthermore, Yin Wood relates to the late spring, leaves and flowers and grass, none of which are obviously feline attributes. By the way, the song "Year of the Cat" written by 1945 Rooster Al Stewart in the Rabbit (*not* Cat) Year of 1975 illustrates again the misunderstanding that often occurs between Rabbit and Rooster. How will the Rabbit fare in a Rooster year? Typical are disappointments and letdown; lowered sights are in order.

## The Dragon

**Who Is a Dragon?**

**Years:** 1940, 1952, 1964, 1976, 1988, 2000.

**Month*:** April

**Hour:** 07.00–09.00

**Day:** You'll need a Chinese Calendar.

**What Is a Dragon?**

The Dragon is Yang Earth, the most egotistical of the branches as well as perhaps the most powerful. Putting aside conventional rules of animal compatibility, many of us are either fascinated by the Dragon or suspicious. Or both. Shameless mischief-maker Vladimir Putin and Trump tribute act Boris Johnson are Dragons. So, however, is Marianne Williamson, whose Presidential ambitions may be over but whose influence continues to grow. It was she who wrote Nelson Mandela's mantra:

> *Our deepest fear is not that we are weak. Our deepest far is that we are powerful beyond measure. It is our light not our darkness that most frightens us.*

This is someone who understands power. Dragons are powerful people Dragon has the ability to transform things with a word or a wave of the hand: possibly the most powerful Animal, but be aware that the Dragon is not always issued with a moral compass. He or she may take a lifetime locating it. Indeed some say they have spent lifetimes already.

The Dragon is effortlessly charismatic, just as charming and affable as (s)he feels like being at any given time, but like the Pig, the Horse and the Rooster, they suffer the *self-clash* which makes them unsuited to working with their contemporaries.

---

* Caution: Chinese months can start as early as the 4th and as late as the 9th.

Dragon school years (kids all born in 2000 or 2012 for instance) are an interesting study, tending to include many inspired individuals who aren't keen on cooperation.

Dragons often live alone and enjoy their own company. Sometimes they claim to even when they don't. Often what she experiences as joy is a subtle experience that others find puzzling. The Horse for instance who likes to dance on tables, may consider the Dragon a high maintenance prima donna. Even his ally the Monkey, contrasts his own goonish delights with the impassive Dragon and can make no sense of him.

And yet the Dragon delivers. Sometimes awkward and gauche, the Dragon can appear incompetent and yet still win. Steadfast Dogs whose workings lead to a logical answer detest this about the Dragon and may sabotage him. Put simply, the Dog thinks the Dragon goes on a bit. The Ox and the Sheep share something of this attitude but are more passive about it. If you are a Dragon, know this: you are likely to induce jealousy. However gracious you are, they know the level of your self-esteem. The life lesson of the Dragon is often, knowing the dominance of his own ego, to give others plenty of respect for theirs.

The Chinese ideogram for thunder is a Dragon under a raincloud. And all over the world rainclouds speak of plenty; drenched is good if you're looking for growth. The Dragon month is April, the time of sudden change. Dragon times are the tense moments before a storm breaks and those moments of release after. This is transformation.

The Dragon does not naturally co-operate or share confidences. He will, however, work with those he considers his inferiors as long as they are very clear about the pecking order. This is the central weakness of the unbalanced Dragon. Maybe King Lear was a Dragon, where Othello may have been a Tiger and Hamlet more of a Snake.

The Dragon's traditional partners are the hands-on Monkey and the plotting Rat although these three may not mix socially.

They need a task to cooperate upon in order to connect. Socially the Dragon will often seek out the Rooster and the Horse both of whom can act as PR or spokesperson. Alone or teamed-up, the Dragon is just as creative as he wants to be. She can magic up wealth and as rapidly squander it. Neither Horse nor Rooster is much help to them in this regard although a benevolent Rat and a diligent Monkey can be.

Dragon and Snake form the *House of Magic.** Dragon is the Sorcerer, the Snake his apprentice. Merlin was a Dragon and his story illustrates the other central weakness of the Dragon: that he can be beguiled by the glamour typical of the Rooster. In a Rooster year the Dragon may forget carefully laid plans and go off-piste, tempted – typically – by wealth or sex. In a Pig year they may have to re-think their approach to life ready for the boom times of the Rat year that follows. In an Ox Year there are break-ups.

A timid Rabbit can piggy-back on the Dragon's fearlessness. In Chinese folklore the Dragon is said to lose wealth in the presence of the Rabbit. This may be an explanation of the *Harm* that persists between these two because of their differing attitudes to the Dog. For the Rabbit the Dog is Secret Friend, protector and guide, the typical Dragon often thinks of the Dog as lumpen and obstructive which may make them naturally inimical to the Rabbit.

Which brings up an important lesson: we learn this stuff to be more conscious, wiser and more helpful. To decide as a Dragon that Dogs are a no-go area is probably an error. Best perhaps to know that you will have instinctive reactions to each other and to aim to be bigger than those reactions. You can't write off 8% of the world that way.

**Note to Employers**: A Dragon employee is the best there is if the task suits him. It had better suit him because he will do precisely what he feels like either way.

**Final Note**: As I said the typical Dragon has to seek his own moral bearings. Which means that unbalanced Dragons are the worst: take alleged predators Philip Green, Jeffrey Epstein and Harvey Weinstein. Who'd have thought these three shared Ba Zi charts?!? Or that they could justify the unjustifiable for so long? Of course as these guys show, the Dragon has the luck of the Devil – technically this is called *fiu gong* and calls for a preventative calculation.

**A Note About Timing**: as you learn to draft a Ba Zi you may sometimes have to make judgement calls as to which Animal a Pillar falls into. Getting the Hour Pillar correct can be critical: if you are presented with a precise hour such as 9 a.m., I recommend caution. The odds are that the midwives did not consider the needs of astrologers before the wellbeing of the new born. This usually means the actual moment of birth was just before the hour struck: in the above case a Dragon Hour rather than a Snake. On the other hand we do need to correct for political interference such as Daylight Saving; in the UK all clocks are an hour fast from April to October. And beware international datelines: Barack Obama was born in Hawaii where many clocks are set to California time. Real time in Hawaii, however, is an hour behind. Failure to make the necessary adjustment may be why many pundits picked McCain for President in 2008. If you're absolutely stuck there's a whole section in Kwok Man Ho's *Authentic Chinese Horoscopes* on the nature of the subject according to Hour of Birth. For myself if I'm sufficiently in tune, I can feel into it. You can learn to do this and of course you can calibrate by asking the subject questions about what happened when. Many masters rely on such calibration.

## The Snake

**Who Is a Snake?**

**Years:** 1941, 1953, 1965, 1977, 1989, 2001.
**Month*:** May
**Hour:** 09.00–11.00
**Day:** You'll need a Chinese Calendar.

**What Is a Snake?**

The Yin Fire Snake sits between the Horse and the Dragon, possibly the most powerful pair of animals in the Zodiac and certainly among the most difficult stools to fall between. So a typical weakness of the Snake is indecision. Next to that is lack of commitment and finally a propensity for sudden and uncharacteristic dishonesty. The Snake is Yin Fire, more about light than heat. Ultimately her mission is the spreading of light but she can easily get lost on the way.

There are perhaps old souls and younger souls. The younger Snake often has a vivid imagination and an inconsistent relationship with the truth; the older Snake may treat Truth as sacred. And Snakes being of Candle Flame Fire, can be easily discouraged. Sometimes they should be actually. Some Snakes stick long term with an inappropriate choice so as to put off making any choice at all.

The most written about Snakes in the third decade of the twenty-first century are apt to include Chinese Premier Xi Jinping. Xi, born in 1953, the year of the Snake in the Grass and appointed at a time when the internal tensions in China – between efficiency and self-expression, between industrial wealth and rural poverty and between cohesion and corruption – had never been so stark. Never question his sincerity – he means what he says – but he is likely, like his near-twin Tony Blair, to believe that the more he is opposed by those whose beliefs

* Caution: Chinese months start as early as the 4th and as late as the 9th.

conflict with his own, the more right he must be. For both of these, dictatorship – that is *tianming*, the *Mandate of Heaven* – is the preferable regime because the Snake can so often not tell the difference between their viewpoint and the absolute. Is this the mark of the young soul?

Older souls may include left-wing totem Bernie Sanders. Born a Metal Snake in 1941, his bluntness is typical of the mature or balanced Snake. Perhaps too truthful for his own good – at least career-wise. He might have chosen to be a more obtuse but more successful politician and a lesser human being.

Truth is the defining issue for the Snake. They can vary between the life-long seeker after truth and the fibber but it is truth that runs them.

Typically, squeezed between the two, the choice for the Snake is between opposites: the extroversion of the Horse and the subtlety of the Dragon, instinct and logic, process and end product, long and short term, relationship and freedom, employment or entrepreneurship. In the face of this dilemma, a balanced Snake will often develop sufficient charm to get through without having to make the hard decisions. In Dragon times Snakes are reckoned to find their Teacher.

Typically the Snake of either gender is not the decision maker in relationship. When they marry a Pig this is doubly so; the power of the Pig's uncertain Yin Water may precisely match the delicate Yin Fire of the Snake, often making for stand-offs and provisional decisions. Technically this is a *Clash*, Yin Water against Yin Fire, these two are natural combatants. Rabbit and Snake, however, are said to be especially compatible.

Those decisions the Snake has not made may include the one to be committed to the relationship. The partner of the Snake (best choice probably Ox or Rooster though Monkey woman and Snake man can work) would be well-advised to drag at least this minimum communication from the Snake early on. Interestingly Snakes can despite all this be among the best makers and keepers of relationship of all 60 Animals. But they sure can make it hard for themselves.

One of the advantages of being between the autocratic Dragon and the unruly Horse is that the Snake has her ego in check. Many would consider her wise because what she has to say is well-considered and she never says too much. The Snake can be a brilliant collaborator, especially in a team with the Ox and the Rooster who are in a sense similar to her neighbours: the Rooster is blatant (much like the irrepressible Horse; both are, like it or not, *pure*) and the Ox sticks to the point, while the Snake anchors them to each other. There may be moments of doubt when the Snake's loyalty wavers. At such times, the Snake asks searching questions which should have been settled long ago and then usually re-commits. The high-minded Brutus was probably a Snake. Not Judas though. To know this, grants the Snake both power and integrity. Snakes who know this about themselves earn undying trust.

The Snake can also work with the Dragon in what is called the House of Magic. Only she can subordinate her ego to the extent that the Dragon demands while also keeping up. An ideal Snake vocation is high-level PA. Usually (and wisely) the Snake opts to be number 2 rather than Big Chief.

The Snake often has the intellectual and visual gifts of Fire. She makes a good critic as her judgement is sound and she is not out to destroy egos. She will generally have natural and effortless style too as well as the long and precise memory of an Animal with a Yang Metal Hidden Stem.

The Snake's relationship with the Monkey may best be described as love-hate. Both have hands-on and logical ability and both attract occasional tussles but where the Monkey welcomes an opportunity for mischief, the Snake treats dispute as a regrettable evil. Their conjunction technically turns both to the Water of emotional disclosure. For the Metal Monkey that means opening to a terrifying nakedness, letting go of the masks they may have put up. For the Snake it's similar: the spontaneity and invention of Fire can be immobilized by Water.

When a Tiger appears in such a form as a Tiger-born person or a Tiger month (February), this misunderstanding can turn nasty. In a Dog year like 2018 it was plainish sailing, in the Ox Year 2021 – when the Monkey was for the second consecutive year, favoured – more complex. If there are Monkeys in your friend group, seek them out and try to find common ground. They may save you when the chips are down; it still won't be their priority though.

The Snake is opposed to the Pig and as both are members of the informal group sometimes called the Four Terminals, they can impede each other's movement. Snakes may develop mobility issues in a Pig year and vice versa.

The Snake prefers a short menu and yes/no questions. In a Rat year their Yin Fire may be baffled by the width of choice represented by Yang Water. It's possible that the Snake's dreams will come true only for her to sprint in the opposite direction. Deep communication often has to be wrenched from the Snake and in the Water years of Rat and Pig there is little support for the tight-lipped. In the Ox year that follows, expect just enough Water but not too much. This makes scope for the restricted level of communication the Snake prefers.

**Final health note**: Snakes have a complex relationship with Fire. They are not usually sun-worshippers but often their skin needs just a little regular sun and without it they may fall prey to easily avoided ailments such as vitamin D deficiency. Caution!

**A Note About Dragons and Snakes: The Sorcerer's Apprentice**: The Snake is often called the "Little Dragon" as she is said to possess something of the Dragon's mercurial ability to enchant. In a Snake Year the Dragon is said to find students or followers. And vice versa of course. The Disney cartoon *Fantasia* features an animated telling of the underlying story of Dukas's *Sorcerer's Apprentice*. Mickey Mouse as the apprentice is left by the Sorcerer to mind the shop and starts casting dangerously half-baked spells bringing predictable chaos. The Snake/Dragon relationship pits the powerful but often naïve Dragon and the wily but typically less schooled Snake. They learn much from each other but their intimacy is likely to be short-lived.

## The Horse

**Who Is a Horse?**

**Years:** 1942, 1954, 1966, 1978, 1990, 2002.
**Month*:** June
**Hour:** 11.00–13.00
**Day:** You'll need a Chinese Calendar.

**What Is a Horse?**

The Horse is Yang Fire: the charmer, the extrovert, the hunter and pursuer of the Zodiac. She is rarely caught out despite their high-risk strategy. He has an ego of course but is better able to laugh at himself than for instance the Dragon. Like the Dragon, the Pig and the Rooster though, they cannot generally work with their own kind. The typical Horse is not a deep thinker and his ego can lead him to suppose that no one else is either. And they are hasty, unlikely to fully consider the repercussions of their spontaneous actions. Brexit PM David Cameron, born in the Year of Fire Horse, may be a good example of just that failing.

There tends to be a belief in shortage at work in the Horse. They think they must be the first to the trough if they are to eat. In romance the Horse like the Rooster can be what Leonard Cohen called "a thin gypsy thief". This means his weakness can be a failure to respect boundaries and property because whether it is women, food or money, there is not enough to go round. Of all the animals, the stud Horse and the seductive Rooster are typically the marriage breakers and the home wreckers. This is not inevitable of course. If we know this about ourselves we can make wiser choices. Just because today is a good day to die, it is not necessarily a good day to kill.

The qualities of Fire include sticking and splitting and predictably the Horse is often not great at commitment. The Yin

* Caution: Chinese months can start as early as the 4th and as late as the 9th.

and Yang of this by the way is that a self-aware Horse is the most constant partner there is.

Success matters a great deal to the Horse. He is not generally subtle. It is the winning not the taking part that tends to concern him. Fate can conspire to push someone with the positive aspect of these qualities forward to greatness. Earth Horse Volodymyr Zelenskyy may be a good example of this: trained as an actor, his extroversion is employed as leadership and his need to win harnessed in service to his country. He has been extraordinarily well cast.

The ever-fiery Horse is not keen on Water and especially not on her diametric opposite the Rat. She experiences this element whether expressed as a Rat year, excessive communication or actual Water, as a dampener of enthusiasm. Water slows him down but does not halt him. Indeed it can stimulate them. If ideas are Fire, constructive appraisal is Water: always needed but not always appreciated especially if disproportionate.

Interestingly the Horse's charisma is best expressed either in a team with the other *Plum Flowers*, Rat, Rabbit and Rooster or in a pair with the Sheep. You will often find Sheep and Horse out and about together, the Horse radiating charm and the Sheep reflecting it. This actually is a mutually beneficial partnership; the Sheep is in awe of the sheer daring of the Horse and the reckless Horse may often need grounding, safety and a short-term loan. Horse places the drinks order for his audience and the Sheep pays the tab.

In the Beatles 1942 Horse Paul McCartney was the PR man but the corresponding long-suffering Sheep was George not John or Ringo (both wilful Metal Dragons). This may be the key to their messy break-up; perhaps we can all let Linda and Yoko off the hook now!

Songwriter, singer in a dozen different voices, peerless bass player, it is an interesting fact by the way that perhaps

McCartney's only peer, Brian Wilson of the Beach Boys was born just 2 days after him. There might be something in this Chinese astrology thing after all.

The Horse's home team all of whom have Fire in common, is with the Tiger and the Dog. These are the hunters of the Zodiac: the Tiger kills, the Horse chases, the Dog guards. This support system is the most likely to bring the Horse rewards. On his own he is prone to burn brightly and extinguish early. He'll have a good time though.

The Horse finds the Ox hard work. There is Metal hidden in the Ox which the Horse can turn to his advantage, but the Ox is a winter creature and part-Water which is something your average Horse is wary of. The Ox's preferences often seem humdrum but he is a threat sometimes because he critiques the Horse without asking permission first.

The Horse has visual, imaginative and intellectual gifts but few Horses value them enough to put them to good use. So many of the words we use about the virtue of work illustrate the unwillingness of the Horse to stick at things: harness, yoke, saddle, blinker etc. Again the yin and yang is that a Horse once-committed, never quits – think Boxer in Animal Farm.

A Horse who works with a Snake may achieve greatness because the Snake understands the Horse just as she understands the Dragon; the Snake is smart enough not to compete. In many ways the Snake is the perfect partner but it is more likely the Snake will recognise this than the Horse. Otherwise the Snake suffers in the short term and the Horse in the long.

Racing, partying, playing, the danger is burnout. The challenge for Horses far and wide is to defer gratification long enough that there remains a future. In a Rabbit Year a Horse may feel underpowered. It may feel as if the Yin Wood is not enough to fuel their ambitions.

**A Note About Horse and Sheep, the Gofer's Gofer:** Holmes and Watson, Don Quixote and Sancho Panza, the Sheep serves as amanuensis and fall guy to the Horse. In British politics, Fire Horse David Cameron employed Coalition partner Fire Sheep Nick Clegg just this way. Stupefied by power, Clegg was often referred to as Cameron's lap dog as he broke campaign promise after campaign promise. Theirs was a classic Horse/Sheep relationship: the Horse demands and the Sheep delivers, sometimes even when it is against their own interests.

## The Sheep

**Who Is a Sheep?**

**Years:** 1943, 1955, 1967, 1979, 1991, 2003.

**Month*:** July

**Hour:** 13.00–15.00

**Day:** You'll need a Chinese Calendar.

**What Is a Sheep?**

Idealistic, Yin Earth, not the top getter-onner with others, the balanced Sheep has well-meant judgements about everybody which can sometimes keep her stuck in first gear. For the unbalanced Sheep (July birthday and/or mid-afternoon birth) ambition and foolishness are pretty much the same thing. For the some, Mick Jagger, Keith Richards, Noel Gallagher, however, leveraging affability for fame and fortune is second nature. The Sheep is typically very keen to reflect the zeitgeist. See below for what the most unbalanced Sheep may do with this gift for belonging.

The Sheep, however, is a sheep. She must belong, sometimes at the cost of bending herself out of shape. A spiritual agenda is likely, Sheep take readily to prayer and indeed are often very facile at entering alpha rhythms. If a Sheep features later in a Ba Zi (say Day or Hour) this may indicate a Road to Damascus. Either way the typical Sheep (especially by Year or Day) is well advised to take a nap in the early afternoon.

The balanced Sheep, as well as being an expert judge of people, knows exactly what matters and is not easily diverted from it. The arrangement for instance that Wood Sheep Bruce Willis, his ex Demi Moore and her ex (and Bruce's fishing buddy) Ashton Kutcher came to, whereby they stayed friends and the children avoided becoming conflicted is not usual, either in Hollywood

* Caution: Chinese months can start as early as the 4th and as late as the 9th.

or the world at large but it is typical Sheep behaviour. They can all change partners as often as a Jane Austen cotillion but Bruce gets to see his kids.

Conversely, the value of caution and conservatism is often clear in Sheep relationships. The most obvious of these is with the extrovert spontaneous Horse whose sidekick the Sheep often ends up being. With the Sheep beside him, the Horse's fun may be a little less riotous but he will also stay out of serious trouble. The Horse and Sheep of 1978 and 1979 for instance, may have been a tag team often drinking and clubbing together, those of 2001 and 2002 may prove to be similar. The Sheep may stand back in amazement at the daring of the Horse but is there both to pick up the pieces and to take advantage when these risks bear fruit. The Horse dances on tables, the Sheep ensures a soft landing. The Horse and Sheep of 1990 and 1991 respectively are by the way a very different proposition. They are about to change the world; watch them.

This illustrates a psychological truth: the risk-taking the Sheep shies away from is exactly what attracts them most. Many a desirable partner has rebounded from a Horse only to find a life-long proposition in the Sheep. Read Marianne Faithfull's revealing autobiography if you want to see how this applied to the afore-mentioned Rolling Stones. Don't try this at home, kids.

Placed as the Sheep is before the Monkey in the Chinese Zodiac, they also understand monkey business. Certain school years will be a mix of Sheep and Monkeys. There is generally a certain wariness between them but they can form a creative team: unorthodox but magical, bringing very different gifts to the party. Something similar applies to a Sheep/Monkey marriage.

The Sheep possesses a natural affiliation with the Pig and the Rabbit; a very domestic alliance, the Chinese ideograph for home is a Pig under a roof and the average Rabbit would like the Pig, happily stay home 24/7 if allowed to. The Rabbit is the diplomat and mixer while the inherently versatile Pig takes up the slack of whatever jobs there are to perform. The Sheep's part is to make things secure. She will have ensured for instance that there are no sworn enemies on the guest list. Sheep is an ideal social secretary as well as a resolver of conflict. Psychotherapy is among appropriate career paths. And of course this gift is one that can be abused as we shall see. Certain politicians are masters of its use: consider 1967 Sheep Michael Gove.

The Sheep is subtly passionate, representing the Yin or feminine side of sexuality and so whether male or female, more seducer than chatter up.

Perhaps most interestingly, the Sheep can form a formidable team with the Dog, the Dragon and the Ox. Individually each of these three is somewhat intimidating to her but when this group gathers, her value becomes obvious. She can draw flexibility from the Dog, humility from the Dragon and cheerful co-operation from the autocratic Ox. Above all he ensures peace among them. Note, however, that Sheep, Dog and Ox without the Dragon form the excruciating Bullying Punishment. These three characters together in a Ba Zi are a pretty poor portent.

Even if all they do is make the coffee, the Sheep is a comforter of the insecure. She understands that most barkers never bite and that aggression is simply inverted fear. Just as George Harrison was the Sheep aspect of the Beatles, Lennon and Starr the Dragons, the inevitable Ox was Producer George Martin. Perhaps the charge that Paul was a natural solo is accurate; he's a Horse after all.

The Sheep has disputes with the Rat but generally over issues she has borrowed from another; such disputes generally lack conviction.

Dog and Sheep don't understand one another and form a fragile couple though a shared sense of responsibility and guardianship might bring them together. Such a couple would tend to stay together "for the sake of the children", especially if the children were unplanned.

A final word: the dark side of the Sheep is to leverage gregariousness for power. Brazilian "strongman" Jair Bolsonaro and cynical media mogul Rupert Murdoch don't fit the pattern of the easygoing Sheep at all. But the Sheep needs the herd to be on their side. They have to belong; sometimes even when that involves falsity and betrayal. Donald Trump was born on a Sheep day, making his deepest quality the need for approval. This is not only the Sheep's nature but often their weakness. In this sense the above are not so much "strongmen" as weaklings because their only strength is in the endorsement of the herd. The sensitive Sheep can feel what the crowd want to hear and give it to them. Populism is so much easier than conviction.

**A Note About Key Dates:** It's a quirk of the Ba Zi that one or more of the Four Pillars (five if you include the Life House) may indicate years of big decisions in the subject's life. Fire Rooster Osama bin Laden was born in the Hour of the Metal Snake which is the Year Pillar of the attack on the Twin Towers. British Prime Minister Theresa May whose short-lived premiership centred on the Brexit crisis, was born on a Fire Monkey Day in the Fire Monkey Year of 1956 while the referendum took place in the Fire Monkey of 2016. Those dates may well form the first line of her obituary.

**A Note About Alpha-Rhythms**: some educators teach that 50 minutes study followed by 10 of consideration is one of the most powerful methods of anchoring learning. There is certainly something in this, most particularly for the Sheep who often has a natural ability to enter the receptive, meditative, alpha rhythm state, a place some describe as between prayer and visualisation. Masters of Ba Zi sometimes teach this explicitly, some simply by example; for the Master of Qi Men Dun Jia (the cutting edge of Chinese divination which is to Ba Zi as 3D chess is to draughts), however, this may be the single most important ability to master.

## The Monkey

**Who Is a Monkey?**

**Years:** 1944, 1956, 1968, 1980, 1992, 2004.
**Month*:** August
**Hour:** 15.00–17.00
**Day:** You'll need a Chinese Calendar.

**What Is a Monkey?**

The image of the Three Wise Monkeys, See No Evil, Hear No Evil, and Speak No Evil is a reasonable summary of the qualities of the Monkey: Yang Metal and a particularly quirky primate. This is typically someone who shrinks from deep involvement. In elemental terms, this often amounts to too much Yang Metal. What is meant by Yang Metal essentially is precision and hence competition. Often the Monkey is so competitive he dare not enter the race.

Competitive yes, often revolutionary, but the Monkey is typically charming, loveable, dexterous, logical, quick witted and exact. The balanced Monkey uses these qualities constructively and in the service of his fellow man. The unbalanced Monkey (with say an August birthday in the late afternoon) does not clean up behind himself. He is in short a monkey.

The Monkey is often the most acquisitive as well as the gentlest beast. In the extreme, of course, competition means warfare. In its milder forms it is the ruthless competition that involves the belief that another's gain is our loss. This is a (painful) mistake. It's what leads to steroid abuse in athletics and ballet dancing in the Premiership penalty box. A Water Monkey like Spurs's Son Heung-Min must have learned this lesson early; Son appears to focus on goals rather than adulation unlike so many Monkeys who subscribe to this

---

* Caution: Chinese month can start as early as the 4th and as late as the 9th.

delusion unless and until they learn not to through hard experience.

And surely learning not to be run by it is one of the main purposes of knowing this stuff? It's a reasonable bet of course that Son knows both himself and his Four Pillars. In some senses traditional Korean culture respected classical Chinese norms more than the Chinese.

As you'd expect, the Monkey's pitfall is frivolity, the Monkey is the sign of the stand-up. If he can't win he takes the Mickey. Their natural allies, however, are the more ponderous Rat and Dragon; a pretty heavy-duty grouping, perhaps the most powerful in the Chinese Zodiac. Dominant Rats and egotistical Dragons are not, as a rule a bundle of laughs; the Monkey, however, usually is.

And together these three get stuff done; so many big revolutions (including those of ideas) involve this team: 1776, 1848, 1944, 1956, 1968 all Monkey years. Monkey revolutions are straightforward upfront affairs, there is no subterfuge. Once they rise there is no ambiguity about where they stand.

The Monkey is as uncomfortable with the Snake, both their Secret Friend and *Harm*, as the Snake is with them. Their combination makes the Water of deep communication, that is to say emotional disclosure and openness but neither is keen to spill the beans.

Monkeys can take issue with Pigs; they have very different ways of working. Neither can see how the other gets anything done. Trust helps.

Monkey for sure is Karen Armstrong author of a *History of God*, founder of the Charter for Compassion and arguably the most important thinker of the twenty-first century. This is a Monkey who has learned to speak no evil while seeing much. If you want to understand forgiveness, the heart of all healing, read Armstrong.

The Monkey tends to understand the Metal of the mechanical: engines and systems; he is the grease Monkey. He can also be gifted at maths, science and argument and suited to a career in engineering or the law, also accountancy. Unbalanced, he neglects all of the above. Even music. The Monkey month of August spans Leo and Virgo and to see him as a hybrid of Virgo control and Leo passion is not far from the truth.

And remember that August is both the month of the Hungry Ghosts and of road rage. Beware the Tiger, Monkey's principal opposition at this time. On Tiger Days (especially during a Tiger year) stay off the roads! Snake Days may not be much better, this is the so-called Fire Penalty. Even Pig days can be affected though usually Pig+Monkey+Tiger+Snake is a constructive moment.

So when the Tiger and the Snake meet the Monkey without a Pig present, there is trouble. The Monkey both co-operates with and fights the Snake. A Monkey-Snake alliance is fragile as neither wants to talk frankly to the other. A Monkey wife might just about contain a Snake husband but the converse is hopelessly volatile. And the presence of the Tiger pushes this competition over the edge. Keep these three apart. The Monkey must take care to mind her p's and q's every February (the month of the Tiger) and every May (the month of the Snake). In years like 2022, 2025 and 2028, the Fire Penalty is a constant: interference, invasion, interruption, unwanted advice, triangular relationships.

So that's the Monkey: argumentative practical, mischievous and so competitive he can withdraw altogether. You might say anything for a laugh but it wouldn't be quite true.

**A Note About the Validity of Astrology**: there are those who insist that astrology is inherently unscientific: an unsupported dismissal which is itself unscientific. There is no question but that the phases of the moon are at least coincident with a woman's menstrual cycle (the words moon, menstrual and month all derive from the same Latin root) tides and the growth of plants. Until it is disproven it is a reasonable conclusion that larger and more distant bodies than the moon may coincide with or cause other effects on Earth. Astrological influences are not unscientific, they are unproven. But to dismiss them without sufficient evidence, actually, is pretty unscientific.

## The Rooster

**Who Is a Rooster?**

**Years:** 1945, 1957, 1969, 1981, 1993, 2005.
**Month*:** September
**Hour:** 17.00-19.00
**Day:** You'll need a Chinese Calendar.

**What Is a Rooster?**

The Rooster is Yin Metal, the night bird, glamorous and with an eye for detail but a short attention span. She appreciates an argument and likes to win but has little patience for causes that drag on. She will appreciate jewellery, fine art and good living and create wealth easily; she can spend it as easily too. Conversely of course, a wide-awake Rooster like Aung San Suu Kyi can reject such distractions in order to serve a cause that has indeed dragged on for decades. And like Aung San Suu Kyi can suddenly and mysteriously change their mind. This is Yin and Yang. The Rooster's moral compass is often a learned thing. Glamorous and fickle are words often associated. *Tsun,* 辛 the character for Yin Metal looks like the stiletto that could as easily end up in your back as adorn a glamorous heel.

The typical Rooster is suited to work such as that of an advocate involving short decisive arguments. Her brief passion is the perfect support for a client. She can defend with 100% commitment and then move on to the next one. If she is in a job that involves holding her peace she may fret and become ill.

Some say the Rooster is simply an attention seeker. Osama bin Laden may be a good example: just the one spectacular splash to his name.

For the Rooster a car must be fast, a partner challenging and life full of twists and turns. The Rooster is likely to be quick

---

* Caution: Chinese months can start as early as the 4th and as late as the 9th, depending on the year.

witted rather than profound, with concentration focused tightly before moving on.

Her allies, the Snake and the Ox, are sometimes impatient with her because she can digress so widely and so easily but she brings to this Metal alliance the pure competitiveness that the Ox might otherwise misuse and the Snake misunderstand. She is pure Metal – who is determined to get it right at all costs. They will not win many cases or many contracts without her and they would do well to pay and respect her appropriately even though she expects longer holidays and more money. A support system that dots t's and attends to punctuation will tend to empower the Rooster's intuitive flashes. She needs a team to generate opportunities which she will exploit. Respect – especially of such a support system – is so often a life lesson. For team read "spouse" by the way.

Her most dangerous pitfalls, however, are sex, drugs and rock'n'roll. They probably like to party to the small hours and their personality may be addictive. They are likely to prefer dusk to dawn.

The Rooster enjoys a powerful alliance with the Dragon in which she may hold the whip hand. This may be unique in the Dragon's experience. They can bend the Dragon out of shape just as the Ox can bend the Rat. This is not always entirely healthy, such sway must be employed responsibly otherwise both can be damaged. With that proviso this is one of the strongest alliances in the Chinese Zodiac.

The Rooster predictably is one of the charismatic Flowers of Romance. Success and glamorous partners come easily to her. Often a Rooster can punch above her weight in this regard. Cinderella appears to have been a Rooster as was Yoko Ono. This effortlessness can make for complacency, bitterness is common among middle-aged Roosters.

Often vanity is a weakness and growing old is hard for her, she can so easily become Snow White's stepmother. Who is the fairest of us all? Consider these aspects in the contrasting lives of Mick

Jagger and Che Guevara, both of whom were born – in different years – on the day of the Rooster. "You're so vain you probably think this song's about you." (Carly Simon 1945 Wood Rooster was clearly concerned with vanity. Why would that be, do you think?)

The Year Animal represents parents among other things. So to say that a woman is a Rooster is to say that her Father was in some sense a Rooster too. It is almost a given that the father of a female Rooster was at least sociable if not a "player". Perhaps this is a socially-induced gender issue but that Yin Metal glamour does tend to play out differently for a male Rooster.

With the Monkey this wily, numerate bird can form a commercial alliance. A business co-run by these two will be irresistible but may not open on time. It may not close promptly either and may suffer the cash flow problems that come from poor financial prioritisation. They'll make lots of money but may spend more. A marriage would risk the same types of problem: great parties, early divorce.

The cautious domesticated Rabbit is the nemesis of the Rooster. The Rooster likes bling and the Rabbit can see no life in a stone. Any close relationship would tend be full of obstruction and passive aggression as well as disappointment and a failure to keep agreements. The insistent Wood of the Tiger is almost as maddening although his fierceness would at least engage the Rooster's attention. The loyal, consistent Dog usually bores her rigid though she may in extremis fall upon him for support.

The Rat is altogether too wordy for the Rooster. The Rat might say too honest. A Rat/Rooster marriage like a similar alliance would tend to break up rapidly.

Some Masters have lists of Pillars that are not suited to marriage. Many of these are Roosters. But, of course, life is for learning and once we know our inclinations we can correct. The smart Rooster plays to her strengths but many don't. Uncorrected, the Rooster may in the words of the Lovin' Spoonful, be "only pretty, what a pity".

## The Dog

**Who Is a Dog?**

**Years:** 1946, 1958, 1970, 1982, 1994, 2006.
**Month*:** October
**Hour:** 19.00–21.00
**Day:** you'll need a Chinese Calendar.

**What Is a Dog?**

The Dog is Yang Earth and a byword for faith and consistency. Terriers and Rottweilers are as fierce as they are loyal. In mediaeval heraldry and Renaissance painting, the greyhound symbolises constancy. The downside of this is that like Donald Trump and two of his three predecessors (ie not Obama – naturally), they can take some moving on. And the primary force in the world in the third decade of the twenty-first century may be the eclipse of the international dispensations of the post-war era which opened in the Fire Dog year of their birth 1946. The search for a new beginning in which humanity has some chance of survival is the counterpoint and in some senses the opposition. Only rejection of the dog-ma of perpetual growth which continues to ravage the planet offers an escape. You may be absorbed with that very question but the Dog remains naturally conservative with a small but stubborn "c".

Dogs revere tradition and tend to have a strong family background. If a Dog commits to something they can generally be relied upon to see it to completion – for better or worse. The difference between male and female Dogs can be that the female gets the message quicker. Interesting to note that Kate Middleton and Prince William are twin Water Dogs of 1982; a very solid match because as a Yang Earth sign, the Dog is pretty immovable, an ideal best friend or protector. It was clear that

---

* Caution: Chinese months can start as early as the 4th and as late as the 9th.

these two were, whatever appears to occur to the contrary, first and foremost good friends.

The Dog's thinking may not always be flexible but when he gets an idea, he really gets it; that's Yang Earth for you. His natural grouping is with the hunters, the Horse and Tiger where the apportionment of tasks is obvious: the Horse provides pace and the Tiger ferocity while the Dog watches the rear. If more people studied Chinese metaphysics, more workplaces would zing: in business the Horse will tend to be the sales person, the Tiger the closer or credit controller and the Dog running after-sales service or HR.

The Dog excels at service because he never gives up. He will return your phone calls and keep that appointment. He's the friend who sends a card every birthday and the spouse who remembers every anniversary. He can be that kind of charmer as well as the Tweeter at dawn.

The Dog perhaps surprisingly, also mixes well with the gentle diplomatic Rabbit. The Rabbit schmoozes while the Dog ensures that her openness is not abused. He makes a wonderful bodyguard and middle manager. A Dog employer will generally have achieved that position by sheer hard work and will demand the same from all around. A Rabbit/Dog marriage is a particularly solid one.

The Dog doesn't like the Dragon because he's such a smarty pants. Dogs tend to disdain success without effort and he sees the Dragon create with such apparent ease. Consider Trump's man-crush on Dragon Vladimir Putin in this light. Doesn't much like the Snake either and the Rooster is altogether too flashy; the Dog would resent the Horse as well, except that they are scrupulously loyal to their own team. And just as an aside, it's a principle of yin and yang that opposites co-exist. So some Dogs will express these qualities in the omission rather than the observance. This may make some little sense of Donald Trump – not known for loyalty to wives, subordinates, gofers or legal representatives.

An unbalanced Dog is a bit of a shop steward. He knows his rights and the way things should be – often the way they always have been. An unbalanced Dog (such as one with an October or mid-evening birth) is rigid. Those recent US Fire Dog Presidents in a downward progress of de-evolution bottoming out at Donald Trump, have been champions of stuck, male, white, wealthy privilege. Make no mistake: it may not be clear very soon but the Fire Dog, the post-War dispensation, is over. The smart Fire Dog has already become mentor and confessor. That's a pursuit at which he can often excel. The shallow Dog of course may never see this.

The Dog will often have a strong spiritual agenda and if he has a blind spot, it may be the inability to tell the difference between religion and spirituality or spirituality and therapy. Any relationship with a Sheep, typically one of the most spiritual Zodiac Animals, is fragile; Sheep need to belong and so does the Dog but to different clubs.

Because this means he sticks to his guns, the Dog is suited both to New Age therapy and religious persecution. He will not be thrown off by the opinions of others once he has committed to a line of action. The unbalanced Dog can be thick skinned in matters of belief; this Dog would be ideally suited to being a Grand Inquisitor. The problem is that her motto is "Do as you would be done by", and she thinks it already is. Resentment is a trap that is so easy to fall into.

The Dog can work well with other Dogs and even with the Pig. With the Pig he shares a love of home and team and they are so different they don't crowd each other. Sometimes the Dog and Pig can be telepathically close; this is because they are adjacent signs in the calendar linked by the Yang Earth that is a feature of both. Sometimes this Earth is expressed by complementary delusions; consider Trump and Earth Pig born-again misogynist Mike Pence. Unfortunately, Pig is Gip Sat, that is delay and obstacle, to Dog. A Dog/Pig marriage would be very fraught and likely, like the Trump/Pence alliance, to end in tears.

But the most powerful and most demanding role the Dog can play is in a creative team including the irritating Dragon, the autocratic Ox and the soft Sheep. If the Dog acts as conscience and bookkeeper, the Ox will relax, the Sheep toughen up and the Dragon acknowledge someone else for a change. If you are a Dog recruiting for non-executive directors, take note. What is great about the Dog is that if he finds advice that works, he will adopt it as if it were religion. Bless. As for the unbalanced Fire Dog – it's pretty much over. Change Horses, I should.

## The Pig

### Who Is a Pig?

**Years:** 1947, 1959, 1971, 1983, 1995, 2007.
**Month***: November
**Hour:** 09.00–11.00
**Day:** You'll need a Chinese Calendar.

### What Is a Pig?

The weakness and the strength of the Pig (who is predominantly Yin Water and therefore often reluctant to communicate) is that they think they know what is good for them. And they are right often enough to make advice close to impossible. By extension this means you Pigs may believe you know what is right for everybody else.

Technically the Pig is a cocktail of Water, Wood and Earth. This makes for extraordinary versatility. But this combined with the Pig's weakness at emotional disclosure can mean that they lack a support system just when they most need one. Consider Fire Pig Hillary Clinton and her rogue email account; the story goes that unable to master her Blackberry, she could not bring herself to seek appropriate help. That's a Pig. The growing wave of mental health issues (for which perhaps read emotional issues) hits the Pig (such as the 1995 Wood Pig) disproportionally hard.

Versatile and wilful, gifted at whatever they do, the Pig is the sign of the inventor. Edison was a Pig and Elon Musk, as is Wikileaker Julian Assange. Perfectly balanced Pigs can literally do almost anything but they don't much like reflective advice from others and they are liable to hate uncertainty. Remember Fire Pig Elton John in "Rocket Man"? And consider Elon Musk's social media tiffs?

---

* Caution: Chinese months can start as early as the 4th and as late as the 9th.

Vagueness is uncomfortable for the Pig: Edison was of course an obsessive patentee, Hillary determined to get Wall Street onside while retaining her liberal credentials. And Assange, confident that he knew better than anyone else what the world needed to know – and maybe he was right. Brexit and the Trumpreich might have fallen differently but for some of these guys. This does not mean they were mistaken but the truth can be a moveable feast.

A balanced Pig (perhaps March birth around mid-afternoon) is a great audience and typically gets the listening/talking ratio just right. An unbalanced one can shoot off at the mouth and give (or take) away the farm before she knows it.

More likely, you are prone to withdrawing into silence. Sometimes the Pig sulks but more commonly withdraws out of pure disinterest and can be perfectly cheerful when challenged on the withdrawal.

The Pig child needs just the right mixture of carrot and stick. Too much disincentive and he is suppressed or resentful. Too much carrot and he can be smug. The balanced Pig is among the most sensitive of the animals; the unbalanced one has undergone an empathy bypass. As the parent of a Pig, just remember you are instrumental in this process. Your Piglet does not need to become a boar.

The Pig harbours the Wood of creativity so they can be as adept with the written as the spoken word and indeed the Yang Earth of deep concentration. Many Pigs prefer to study in noisy rooms and many are effortless A-students as tutors of A-Level students of 2023 may have learned. Bear in mind though that there is a near-epidemic of depression and anxiety among millennials and that Water is the associated element. Don't ever take a 1995 or 2007 Pig's good cheer for granted or their call for help as crying wolf.

The Stevie Smith poem "Not waving but drowning" is about a Pig. They look so competent. And they are. Until they're not. If you care for a Pig beware of their apparent endless confidence. There are crucial gaps. Be there for them before they ask.

Pig does not tend to like Snake; one way or another they immobilise each other; there are mutual issues of trust, truth and sincerity. And the Monkey, Snake's intimate – possibly for that reason – can be annoying too. The Pig's natural team is with Rabbit and Sheep, a quintessentially domestic alliance; together they can make anywhere home. A perfect family might be Pig father, Rabbit mother, Sheep first-born. Once home, the Rabbit entertains while Sheep ensures compatibility, and the Pig performs tasks that are beyond the scope or interest of the others. Monkeys can be too trivial minded to be good company.

Traditionally the Pig does enjoy the company of the Tiger as Elton John's husband, Water Tiger David Furnish, can attest. You might think the Pig would be more cautious but they know that the Tiger is uninterested in conquering anyone he considers easy meat. Of course she's missing something here but the Pig's fearless approach often disarms the Tiger before they realise it. And by the by, Pig's literary ambition often burgeons in a Tiger year and flourishes in a Rabbit one. Some say Pig may fall in love in a Tiger year.

Although she may herself be more adventurous, the Pig also understands the loyal and consistent Dog. She respects the fact that every home needs its guardian. These two may develop a camaraderie with its own distinctive banter but it will probably never be a meeting of souls as Pig is technically the Dog's *gip sat* or force of obstruction. The Pig respects the Dog's diligence and the Dog knows the Pig will compensate for his weakness but they're not exactly comfortable together.

The Pig is also a fine factotum for a group consisting of Snake (whose company she can't otherwise stand for long) the Monkey (ditto) and the Tiger. For these she is, interestingly, the peacemaker and setter of standards. Without the Pig this grouping whose common interest is travel and mobility, can't get off the ground. Once the Pig has settled the Fire Penalty of Tiger, Monkey and Snake, endemic in years like 2022 and 2025, everything works. Taron Egerton who impersonated Elton so effectively in Rocket Man, is a 1989 Snake.

One final note: the Pig suffers what is called the *self-curse.* That is to say that she has limited patience with other Pigs. And as Rocket Man illustrates, a huge capacity for self-loathing. The Chinese character for a house is one Pig under a roof. Just the one. Approach gently and listen carefully.

# Module I: Preparing to Draft the Ba Zi

## 1. Time for Te: Origins, Ba Zi and the Tao

In the beginning is, was, will be the *Tao*.

Ba Zi is not centrally a mechanical process. When I am drafting, I will pay attention to noises just within earshot, a snatch of music, a momentary sentiment, the quality of the light. The universe is talking to us all the time, it's helpful to listen. I aim to be in a semi-hypnotic state, a dream if you will. Some might call it alpha-rhythms. Its central feature is benevolence towards my subject. My aim is to be in tune with the Tao and in service to my client.

The idea of the Tao is extremely old though it only becomes formalised in the final millennium BCE. From the idea of the Tao is derived much of what we might call Chinese metaphysics. Indeed, from the Tao is derived much of what we might call Chinese culture: the *Book of Changes*, Yin and Yang, the *Wu Xing* or *Five Elements* of Wood, Fire, Earth, Metal and Water and hence the *Stems* and *Branches*, the building blocks of the Ba Zi (although these last come to us down a different line of descent, of course). We might include Chinese diplomacy, cuisine, music, business practice and military theory in this list. Many of these ideas have been adopted – some might say hijacked – by other schools of thought over the centuries. We shall be touching on both the history and the legendary accounts of this evolution.

This idea of the Tao, I suggest underlies all things. The Tao is and is not. It is eternal and it is not there at all and never was. It is solid and it is nothing. It is, in the words of Jeff Beck, everywhere and nowhere. When we speak of "trusting the process" we are probably speaking of the Tao (which is hazardous, because Lao Tze – if indeed he existed – tells us in the handbook of Taoist thought – the *Tao Te Ching** – that *the Tao that can be spoken of is not the Tao*). Is it simply then, that of which we cannot speak? Caution: would that not itself be a way to speak of it? The unnameable is itself a name.

Lao Tze was roughly contemporary with Confucius, that is Kung Fu Tze (551–479 BCE). Confucius took the central idea of there being an appropriate moment for and response to all things as being essentially moral. Where Confucius diverges from Lao Tze is that he thought of a settled society as an absolute good and the Tao as a route to it.

The word Tao actually means "way". Some term it the "flow". When we speak of *going with the flow,* it is most likely the Tao that concerns us. The Anglo-Saxon concept of the *wyrd – that which unfolds is the outcome of all that went before** – may be close. Perhaps the Tao being elusive to the mind's logical functions is a glimpse of the infinite. The most appropriate response may be laughter or tears. What's for sure is that the bulk of the body of ideas known as feng shui are intimately connected with this notion of the Tao.

To engage with the Tao can be a risky business. I remember watching a Taoist Master make a fool of himself trying to explain the Tao to a group of young women. It was his insistence that he understood it that wrong-footed him. Indeed, the Tao may serve as a lesson in humility, an illustration that not everything is subject to reason.

Western seekers after truth often think of the Tao as the line of least resistance. Sometimes it is perhaps, but the Tao is not necessarily the open door and not necessarily not the closed one. It may or may not be the downward slope. What appears to be the case is that if we respect the appropriate in our actions and reactions, life is less fraught and more meaningful.

---

* *The Classic of the Way and the Appropriate.* Te means something like *"virtue"* and may correspond somewhat to the Greek *arête* meaning the *"good for man"*. Lao Tze, whose name means something like "Young and Old" was more likely a series of groups over generations than an individual, by the way. # Brian Bates.

Conversely when we attempt to wrest the Tao inappropriately in our preferred direction, upset tends to follow.

The early Chinese diviners could not, we must assume, second-guess the Tao any more than we can. The Tao appears to have no discernible moral – or indeed other – objective, unlike Confucius whose worthy purpose of fostering filial piety and socialised behaviour seems to have blinded him to the amoral, aetiological nature of the Tao. Many educated Chinese to this day believe the Yi to be a book of Confucian homilies, knowing little of its origins or context. Indeed, the same is true of some feng shui Masters.

The Tao being flexible and insubstantial (except of course when it is rigid and substantial) may be where we go in alpha-rhythms. It may be the place where thought becomes visualisation which in turn becomes prayer. It may be the familiar place we go to in our dreams, from which we know we came and to which we know we return. It may be the place where what has been and what is yet to come takes shape. It may be where, if we can access it, the answers to all questions may be located. This makes it perhaps where divination takes place.

We can dip into the Tao in a number of ways. There are many, many methods and many, many words in many, many languages for this pursuit. One of these routes is via the Ba Zi. The formal rules of Ba Zi are drawn from the notions of the *Wu Xing* or "Five Elements" as well as Yin and Yang but the Tao I suggest, provides the ultimate reference.

Consideration of the Tao may allow us to be less rigidly bound by the rules we impose upon ourselves in our daily lives. Such consideration may allow for transformation and miracle in a way that adherence to logic, good sense and gravity may not.

For now and for our purposes in drafting and interpreting Ba Zi, I suggest we treat the Tao as an important reference point.

**The Abbot and the Stones**

The story is told of the Abbot who assembled his students one morning and showed them that he had placed a sequence of stones across the abbey courtyard: nine black, one white; nine black, one white; nine black, one white. As the novices followed the line of stones with their eyes, they found that they could track it beyond the enclosure and out across the valley floor. The stones may indeed have stretched to the valley wall.

They chattered among themselves trying to make sense of it.

"Nine is Fire, one is Water," one said.

"Nine and one are Mother and Father," said another.

"He must have been up all night," said a third who was at that stage in his education that it was close to time for him to leave and find fresh learning. Such a stage is often one of growing disrespect.

"Tell me," the Master asked gently, "if that line of stones were infinite what would be the ratio of black to white stones?"

"Nine to one of course," the disrespectful student retorted. There was a gasp at his tone.

"No," said the Master, "if the line of black and white stones were infinite their numbers would be exactly equal."

## 2. One Hand Clapping, the Big Bang: Yin and Yang

Scientists tell us that the Universe is around 13.7 billion years old, which begs the question: what came before? This question can perplex. Similarly, they say the Universe is expanding at a measurable rate. Where is it going? And what is beyond that? These certainties sound, on the face of it, as if they tell us something ultimate. But do they?

According to tradition, at some point in time (whatever that means) the Tao gives birth to matter. First there is the *mo chi* – the Great Singularity – and then all at once there is *Yin* and *Yang*: dark as well as light, action as well as reaction, caves and protrusions, round and square.

**Yin** is darker, slower, heavier, more rounded, less outgoing, more empowering than active, subtle and essentially feminine. The night is often considered Yin, as are the moon and the Ocean.

**Yang** is lighter, brighter, more rapid, more protrusive, extrovert, aspirational, unsubtle, essentially masculine. The day is often considered Yang, as are the sun and the forest.

These qualities pervade and define all there is. Nothing is pure yang or pure yin and everything that is Yang is Yin in comparison to some other things, as all that is Yin is Yang in comparison to some other things.

And the idea of yin without yang is of course as meaningless as the sound of one hand clapping. How could there be one without the other? The Universe appears to consist exclusively of complementary qualities.

In this mythical account of the origin of things, following undifferentiated yin and yang in the *mo chi,* we first have *tai* (or *great*) *yang* and *tai yin,* a preliminary separation. Then we have *xiao* (or small) *yang* and *xiao yin.* Then instantaneously the yin mixes with the yang and we have the myriad or 10,000 things. Everything flickers into being, every object, flower, beast, thing and article, each a complex of yin and yang.

## 3. Elements and Elementals: Cycles and Psychology

The *wu xing, Five Elements* or Five Agents – Earth, Metal, Water, Wood, and Fire – were first described as "Elements" by lazy Western observers who thought that since Empedocles's ultimate components of reality (Earth, Fire, Air and Water) shared three terms with the wu xing, they must be the same. Many modern authorities would disagree. Better translations of "Elements" include terms such as: phases, intersections, movements, acts, paths, career, developments, changes.

In fact, it's pretty clear that the Five Elements correspond to the Five Visible Planets (Jupiter, Mars, Saturn, Venus, Mercury) whose observable colours are respectively greeny-blue (that is Wood), red (Fire), brown (Earth), white (Metal) and black (Water) and which rise in that order. And this again is related to the ten-day week of the earliest Chinese calendar and thus to the Ten Celestial Stems.

The Elements identified by the Greek natural philosophers were static things. The whole essence of the wu xing is that they are not. Similarly, Empedocles saw his elements as irreducible and therefore separate. The wu xing, however, like yin and yang, cannot exist independently and are defined by how they interact. Metal in a sense is simply something that emerges from the Earth, is melted by Fire, when in its molten state it is Water and once solid again can shape Wood. On another level Metal is precision; no other substance can be measured to a tolerance of microns. Consider for a moment perhaps whether Metal would mean anything at all without Water, Fire, Earth and Wood.

Having dismissed that line of thought, it's reasonable to speculate that the theory of the "Humours" propagated by the Graeco-Roman Galen, Godfather of medical theory comes via significant corruption, from a source in common with Elemental theory. Again, the advantage Chinese culture has over all others is having been functionally unbroken since the Qin (221–206 BCE).

The relationships between the Elements each fall into one of three cycles, that of production, destruction or exhaustion. And each Element has a unique relationship with each of the others. It's a little like the children's game of rock, paper, scissors.

Another way perhaps of looking at the wu xing is that they are a fine-tuning of the ideas of Yin and Yang; immovable mountainous, inert Earth is as Yin as things get. Dynamic sparking Fire approaches total Yang, so does the restless motion of great bodies of Water. And yet the most Yin thing is Yang compared to something else and vice versa. So there exist both Yin Fire and Yang Earth. Meanwhile, the ultimate Yang of Fire ends with the near-total Yin of desert and ash, while at the extreme of earth is Earth, the ever-moving yang rotation of the planet itself. The principle of yin and yang is like an acorn that contain forests of ideas.

Let's make clear at this point that pretty much everything in authentic Chinese feng shui is based either on the relations between the Elements (e.g., Ba Zi) or on the Trigrams of the *Book of Changes*. Methodologies, interpretations, formulae and additions have been developed that are useful and powerful, but that remains the case. You may find this bold statement comforting when you are confused as to what is and what is not feng shui and more to the point, what is and is not Ba Zi.

## The Interactions of the Five Elements, Phases or Agents, the Wu Xing, Their Interactions and the Heavenly Stems

The Taoist method is essentially one of observation. Although early physicians were apparently permitted to examine corpses on the battlefield, the vast body of anatomical knowledge that accreted to the study of acupuncture was achieved largely without dissection. The theory of the relations between the Elements, which acupuncture has in common with Ba Zi, appears to have been observed in a similar way.

As we have learned the Gan Zi Cycle unites two early systems of time measurement: the Stems and Branches. We have learned about the origins of the Branches in the observations of proto-Taoists and the derivation of the Stems from an early Chinese system of 10-day weeks, which gives us the familiar Cycle of Production which of course runs Water, Wood, Fire, Earth, Metal and so on, not quite like the sequence of the Branches where Earth is central in a different way.

This is the Cycle of Time.

**The Sequence of the Elements (aka the Cycle of Production)**

**Water** is fluid and without shape. Its direction is downwards. It is as flexible as anything can be but it cannot be compressed. In its yin form, it is easily dried up, in its yang form inexhaustible. Unless it is interfered with, all Water on the planet is connected with all other Water and shares a single level. Accordingly, Water represents communication and adaptability, danger, traps, pitfalls and the Second Son.
**Water** *produces* **Wood** just as a tree requires Water.
**Water** *drains* **Metal** just as melting leads to setting.
Another way to say this is that **Water** is produced by **Metal.**
**Water** *destroys* **Fire** by quenching it. **Water** is *destroyed* when **Earth** pollutes it.

**Wood** is expansive and flexible but not infinitely so. It grows up, down and outward constantly. In its yang form, Wood can be an obstruction, it goes wherever there is Water, Fire and Earth. Accordingly, Wood represents movement, growth, the will and healing, ambition, aspiration, and both the Eldest Daughter (yin) and the Eldest Son (yang).
**Wood** *produces* **Fire** just as striking a match does.
**Wood** *drains* **Water** just as a watering can is emptied.
Another way to say this is that Wood is produced by Water.
**Wood** *destroys* **Earth** by exploiting it. **Wood** is *destroyed* when **Metal** fashions it.

**Fire** destroys, consumes and warms. Its action is earthly but its power is from Heaven. Its direction is upwards. Yin Fire illuminates before it heats while the reverse is true of Yang Fire. Accordingly, Fire represents curiosity and fame, publicity, social climbing and the Second Daughter.
**Fire** *produces* **Earth** just as conflagration leaves ash.

**Fire** *drains* **Wood** just as a fire exhausts fuel.
Another way to say this is that **Fire** is produced by **Wood**.
**Fire** *destroys* **Metal** by making use of it. **Fire** is *destroyed* when **Water** suppresses it.

**Earth** is still. Earth is solid. In its yin form, it is fertile, the source of life. Yang Earth, however, is remote and massive. Accordingly, Earth represents loyalty as well as stubbornness, birth and bulk, the Mother (yin) and the Youngest Son (yang).
**Earth** *produces* **Metal** just as the Earth produces ore.
**Earth** *drains* **Fire** just as ash is its residue.
Another way to say this is that **Earth** is produced by **Fire**.
**Earth** *destroys* **Water** by polluting it. **Earth** is *destroyed* by nourishing **Wood**.

**Metal** can be either solid or fluid. Its direction is inward. It is most easily fashioned when liquid. Yang Metal can be a dangerous weapon. As jewellery, in its yin form, it is glamorous. Metal can be sharp or dull and take any shape but once fashioned, Metal is not usually easy to change. Accordingly, Metal represents rules and competition, proportion, authority, beauty and precision, the Father (yang) and the Youngest Daughter (yin).
**Metal** *produces* **Water** as Metal is fashioned when molten.
**Metal** *drains* **Earth** just as it is drawn from the ground.
Another way to say this is that **Metal** is produced by **Earth**.
**Metal** *destroys* **Wood** by cutting it. **Metal** is *destroyed* by giving **Fire** purpose.

## 4. Divination for Fun and Prophet: Interpreting the Waking Dream

The Universe is always talking to us, if we are prepared to listen.

Divination is the process by which we inform ourselves of this; anything we wish to know about the universe and especially that knowledge to which we might not otherwise gain access, is available if we are paying attention.

Technically there are two forms of divination: *impetrative* and *oblative*. Impetrative is where we specifically request knowledge. The oblative arrives at our feet whether we have requested it or not. The Trojan seer Cassandra, for instance, was the victim of oblative divination. She was given answers (which you will recall nobody believed) whether she raised questions or not. The wooden horse which she knew to be fatal, appeared on Troy's doorstep without her bidding. Avoiding a black cat or walking under a ladder are very simple forms of oblative divination.

Hexagram Four (*Meng*, that is *Youthful Folly,* Mountain over Water) of the *Book of Changes* makes this distinction clear. The Hexagram gently rejects the seeker of answers, pointing out that the "inexperienced" has sought the Tao and not the other way round. Consider for a moment the folly of attempting to drag a Mountain over Water.

The Ba Zi, like feng shui, clearly falls into the impetrative category. That is to say that in drawing up the characters we are setting up the conditions to gain answers we might access no other way, to questions that are beyond reasoning. This is precisely the process that led the Zhou and Shang diviners to the development of much of what became feng shui theory, probably including the notion of Yin and Yang.

Much has been made in twentieth-century Philosophy (often indicatively called *analysis*) of the distinction between dreaming and waking. This has led to breakthroughs in human consciousness. An example might be Carl Gustav Jung's work on dreams. Divination by contrast involves treating the two states as if they were identical. To the Diviner the notion that such knowledge is arrived at only during sleep is a dreadful waste. We might call divination "the interpretation of the waking dream".

Jung, by the way, who said that he did not believe in God but *knew* God, wrote the introduction to the standard (Wilhelm/Baynes) translation of the *Book of Changes*.

**A Note About Divination:** Although the universe talks to each of us, diviners vary as to what and how much information they need. Some can draw remarkable conclusions from cloud formations, the flames of a fire and indeed crystal balls. You might categorise Ba Zi as simply complex divination.

The *Book of Changes* or *Yi* (aka *I Ching*) can be extraordinarily informative and can provide information without any prompting. Indeed, on 23 June 2016, my wife, Sheila, and myself were on our way to vote in the Brexit Referendum at around 8 in the morning. Which is of course the time of the school run and so we found ourselves in heavy traffic. As it happened, for 15 minutes or so we were stuck in second gear behind a car with a number plate that could be interpreted thus: the first three letters of the number plate corresponded to the Hexagrams of the Yi, the fourth numeral corresponded to "Union", the final letters corresponded to "not". (To protect the identity of the vehicle, I am unable to quote the number plate.)

"Not looking good," I said to Sheila. And so it turned out.

## 5. The Gan Zi or Jia Tze Cycle

### *A. Accelerating Our Learning: The Ten Heavenly Stems*

For myself, I entered the world of Chinese Metaphysics from the direction of alternative psychology. My principal models were Jungian Psychology, Chuck Spezzano's Psychology of Vision™ *A Course in Miracles* and Neuro-Linguistic Programming, one of whose tributaries is the study of accelerated learning. The key to AL is identifying what knowledge is optional and what is essential. Another way to express this is an awareness of when recognising the tip of an iceberg of information saves you learning the whole iceberg by rote. This means concentrating on principles and patterns rather than the example – which is not actually the method of most feng shui Masters I have studied with. In many fields of learning, less of the information presented is essential than you think.

The Greek philosopher Euclid proposed a mere nine principles from which all mathematics (and indeed physics) is derived. If Chinese Metaphysics were similarly reduced to the smallest possible number of pieces of information (about thirty-seven, I think, by the way) from which everything else including all formulae, procedures and cures can be derived, it would include all Ten Heavenly Stems. That is how important they are. As you will discover, the Branches or Animals (which you will also need to know) are actually made up of Stems.

*For the time being at least this knowledge also releases you to ignore all Chinese terms and characters, other than the twenty-two Stems and Branches as interesting and colourful, but unimportant unless they are flagged as essential.*

Remember, however, that the essential information about the Ten Heavenly Stems includes the sound of each character as well as the pictures inherent in the written ideograph. Since both feng shui and Ba Zi are on one level divination, as we have discussed, we need to be facile with the information from which we divine. To know only polarity (yin or yang) and elemental nature (Water, Wood, Fire, Earth, Metal) will seriously limit this ability. If we know not only what the Ten Heavenly Stems mean but what they sound and look like as well as their origins, we have significantly more to play with. But as I say, there is a maximum of thirty-seven characters and only twenty-two you need to know right away. And you will develop your own relationship with each over time.

### The Gan Zi Cycle of 60 Pillars

As we have learned 2023 was ruled by the Water Rabbit. Such composite Zodiac Animals or Pillars consist of a Heavenly Stem (see below) and an Earthly Branch.

2022
壬 - Water (Heavenly Stem)
寅 - Tiger (Earthly Branch)

And since Yang Water is followed by Yin Water, Yin Water by Yang Wood and, as you know, Tiger by Rabbit and Dragon, the next three Year Pillars in the Gan Zi Cycle following the Cycle of Production and the order of the Branches, are Water Rabbit (2023), Wood Dragon (2024) and Wood Snake (2025):

2023 Water Rabbit
癸 - Heavenly Stem
卯 - Earthly Branch

2024 Wood Dragon
甲 - Heavenly Stem
辰 - Earthly Branch

2025 Wood Snake
乙 - Heavenly Stem
巳 - Heavenly Stem

I will describe each Pillar as we proceed. For now, simply absorb that they fall into a cycle of 60, starting with the Wood Rat (甲子) and ending with Water Pig (癸亥) The 60 Year Cycles fall into further "Ages" of 180 Years, as we shall discover and there exist further longer cycles that need not concern us here. And above all, remember that this cycle rules equally the sequence of Months, Days, Hours and indeed Minutes as well as Years.

This sequence is reckoned to have been in use since 2637 BCE. If you count back, you'll find that that year is a Wood Rat which for most purposes is considered the first in the sequence.

## The Ten Heavenly Stems

The Stems are very ancient indeed. There is no question that the earliest Chinese writers were the diviners and that what they wrote included several characters we will be using. The Stem characters – which are used to give an Elemental value to each Animal – are at least three thousand years old and may be more like eight thousand. *Ding* (丁) for instance is so ancient that its meaning is clearly pre-linguistic let alone pre-literary.

Ding, sometimes called "Candle Flame" is Yin Fire. Literally, a nail, nettle or clove, it also carries the meanings *stick* and *split*. It remains open to speculation as to how these opposed significances came to coexist. What is remarkable is that these three meanings apply to the word *clove* in English: it signifies a pungent vegetable as well as the meanings "to cleave to" (as in the Wedding Service) and to *cleave apart* as in *meat cleaver* or *cloven hoof*.

This triple correspondence is hard to explain other than in extraordinarily ancient cultural connections. Similar multiple significances apparently apply to a (Gothic) rune *leuk* (which has come down to us in words such as garlic and leek) that was used as a charm around the time of the Birth of Christ, again suggesting pre-linguistic correspondences. These are clearly very ancient characters and for sure significantly older than the Branches, as will become clear.

### The Ten Heavenly Stems

| | 甲 | 乙 | 丙 | 丁 | 戊 |
|---|---|---|---|---|---|
| **Cantonese** | gap | yute | bing | ding | mow |
| **Pin Yin** | jia | yi | bing | ding | wu |

| | 己 | 庚 | 辛 | 壬 | 癸 |
|---|---|---|---|---|---|
| **Cantonese** | gay | gung | tsun | yum | quai |
| **Pin Yin** | ji | geng | sin | ren | gui |

There are only ten pieces of new knowledge here. Learn their names and qualities. Repeat the names over to yourself. Draw them. It is at this stage of almost no importance to pronounce them correctly or to form them in a way that a calligrapher would approve of. You may in time choose to hone these skills but for now that, I suggest, is window-dressing. Do consider what each character looks like to you. This may help you remember them and it will certainly add to your ability to use them. In divination, your opinion is always valid and imagination is often your best ally. Ba Zi is all about meaning.

**Monkeys, Hands and Seeds**

What the characters mean to you is at least as important as their traditional significances.

The fact for instance that *gap/jia* 甲 (Yang Wood) to many of us resembles 申 (*Shen* the Monkey) is both helpful and meaningful. One tradition* is that 甲 started out as a representation of a seed ready to burst out of the ground while 申 actually depicts a hand or hands. You may see these images in the characters, or you may not. You may see something else altogether. A target? A window? A fan?

When they appear together in the Wood Monkey – 甲申 – many interpreters infer a decision hanging in the balance. This is in the elemental values but also visible in the pictures. Can you see this or do they mean something entirely different to you? This is pure divination. And your view is valid, however new you are to the subject.

* Another is that each is derived from an asterism on the Ecliptic.

## The Elemental Values of the Ten Heavenly Stems

| | 甲 | 乙 | 丙 | 丁 | 戊 |
|---|---|---|---|---|---|
| **Cantonese** | gap | yute | bing | ding | mow |
| **Pin Yin** | jia | yi | bing | ding | wu |
| **Element** | wood | wood | fire | fire | earth |

| | 己 | 庚 | 辛 | 壬 | 癸 |
|---|---|---|---|---|---|
| **Cantonese** | gay | gung | tsun | yum | quai |
| **Pin Yin** | ji | geng | sin | ren | gui |
| **Element** | earth | metal | metal | water | water |

Notice the elements appear in pairs. Notice also that they are in the sequence of the Cycle of Production. Another way to say this is that their order reflects that of the year or the day. First there is the budding of spring which is Wood, then the heat of the Fire in summer. Then there is the Earth which is the dust that remains after great heat which is followed by the Metal grey shadows of evening and of autumn. And finally, the liquid cool and dark Water of night.

**The Elemental Values and Polarity of the Ten Heavenly Stems**

Notice that the Yang character appears first. Broadly, Yang represents birth and newness and broadly Yin represents maturity and decay. So, this makes sense. One of the most attractive aspects of Chinese Metaphysics is that it all fits together perfectly. Like mathematics it has an inevitable order which many would call beautiful. It is like a vast jigsaw puzzle into which each piece slots perfectly. There are exceptions and wild cards but Ba Zi is essentially made up of patterns.

| | 甲 | 乙 | 丙 | 丁 | 戊 |
|---|---|---|---|---|---|
| **Cantonese** | gap | yute | bing | ding | mow |
| **Pin Yin** | jia | yi | bing | ding | wu |
| **Element** | wood | wood | fire | fire | earth |
| **Polarity** | yang | yin | yang | yin | yang |

| | 己 | 庚 | 辛 | 壬 | 癸 |
|---|---|---|---|---|---|
| **Cantonese** | gay | gung | tsun | yum | quai |
| **Pin Yin** | ji | geng | sin | ren | gui |
| **Element** | earth | metal | metal | water | water |
| **Polarity** | yin | yang | yin | yang | yin |

**A Note About Music**: As I've said elsewhere, I think of the Ba Zi principally as a powerful healing device. Tears are very often a sign of such healing. The playwright Willy Russell (author of *Blood Brothers* and *Shirley Valentine*) once told an interviewer that he never played music while he was writing because he wanted to be sure any emotional effect was down to his words not the music. For something like the opposite reason, I almost always play emotive music when I am drafting. I want to find the *qing*, the poignance that may be hidden within the Ba Zi. It's almost always there and once discovered is very likely to lead to tears – mine and those of the subject – when I debrief the Ba Zi with them. And tears are so often the bridge to healing.

## *B. The Animals of the Zodiac: The Twelve Earthly Branches*

### When the Year Begins

Not all Ba Zi Masters agree on the moment that the Year Animal changes. There are three major views on this. And as we progress, we will consider all three.

The tradition of naming the Twelve Earthly Branches after animals was introduced by Buddhist monks around the sixth century CE. The legend has it that the Twelve Animals were invited by the Buddha to delineate the calendar. The Tiger would cover February which was to begin the year, the Rabbit March and so on. There was a bit of a squabble between the Eagle and the Rat. So much, so cute, there is of course more to it.

The light, that is the sun, almost dies and is reborn at *dung gee* (the Winter Solstice) and so that day is in some sense the beginning of the Animal Year; perhaps 20% of practitioners treat the Solstice as such and there is considerable historical authority for that view.

However, the fresh energy of the year is not obvious much before spring, so the opening day of the Tiger of February is quite a practical point to start. That day, the Spring Festival or *Lap Chun* falls on or about 4 February and opens the new Animal Year for around 40% of Ba Zi practitioners. The Qing Emperor Qian Long (1733–93) actually enforced this choice.* But its derivation from dung gee is clear: it is precisely three Solar Fortnights later.

The remaining approximately 40% of Ba Zi Masters reckon the Year from the beginning of the first Lunar Month, tellingly, also derived from the Solstice, falling on the second new moon after it (which can be as early as 22 January or as late as 23 February).

---

* As explained by Thomas Aylward as *The Imperial Guide to Feng Shui & Astrology*.

Interestingly, the *Book of Changes* places the all-yin Hexagram *Kun* around the Solstice:

☷ **Earth** over
☷ **Earth**

As you can see, this Hexagram (i.e. six-line diagram) consists exclusively of broken lines. It is as open, as dispersed, as close to death as it is possible to get, there is like the Solstice almost no light in it. Kun is often called the *Empowering* or the *Receptive.*

As Lao Tze wrote: *Solidity is an advantage but it is emptiness that makes a vessel useful.* This of course emphasises the role of divination, that is to say individual interpretation; to place the cut-off at dung gee in line with the oral tradition, is generally my preference but you will over time and by experimentation conclude as to which works best for you and when.

I respect a cusp between Solstice and Spring Festival, but I think by calculating from the Solstice we may obtain an insight into heart, soul and psyche that we might miss working from the later cut-off dates. The Chinese have historically used feng shui and Ba Zi for the material outcomes of wealth and power, so it may be that the more blatant information of the spring-based Ba Zi suits them better.

As I say, over time you will develop your own view.

### The Year Animals

The ideographs of the Earthly Branches hardly appear elsewhere in Chinese culture and it may be that some are not Chinese in origin. There is a relatively widely held view that Fu Xi, the introducer of the Trigrams (three-line diagrams) two of which make up each Hexagram of the *Book of Changes* was not Chinese at all. There is a not-so widely held theory that Fu Xi was a proto-Celt and some of the correspondences between the ancient Turkic and Chinese cultures may record this. Some authorities (such as Derek Walters) consider this wildly speculative.

Be that as it may, the animal identities appear to have been introduced to summarise qualities that are actually a mixture of several elements and polarities. Each is a unique idea that has been carefully selected to represent both a time and a place. As there are twelve, their distribution is tidier than the Stems (at least across the year and the day) and it is clear how each relates consistently to a particular Chinese month and double hour. How and why the branches relate to days and years may not immediately be so obvious.

Here they are:

**The Twelve Earthly Branches**

| | | | | | |
|---|---|---|---|---|---|
| **Rat** | **Ox** | **Tiger** | **Rabbit** | **Dragon** | **Snake** |
| 子 | 丑 | 寅 | 卯 | 辰 | 巳 |
| chee | chou | yan | muw | shun | jee |
| tze | chou | yin | muw | zhen | si |
| **Horse** | **Sheep** | **Monkey** | **Rooster** | **Dog** | **Pig** |
| 午 | 未 | 申 | 酉 | 戌 | 亥 |
| ng | may | shen | yuw | sute | hoi |
| wu | wei | shen | yuw | su | hai |

As the Buddhist monks have done this work for us, it is perfectly reasonable to refer to the branches by their animal names in English. If similar shorthand were available for the Stems the subject would in point of fact be markedly easier. Having said this, again there is information in the way the characters are written as well as in the Chinese names. Learn to draw them and know the Chinese names; the discrepancy between the Cantonese (top) and Pin Yin terms is much more slight than with the stems. This is at least partly because the Branches are much younger terms. The Stems which make them up may be many thousands of years old, as we discussed, which suggests by the way that knowledge of the principles of feng shui may once have been universal. It may be that feng shui is thought of as Chinese simply because the Chinese is the only civilisation on earth that has been unbroken from inception and that, therefore or otherwise, their records are better than anyone else's.

Again, there is information in the structure of the ideographs. The character 戌 (**Dog** sute/xu) for instance is almost indistinguishable from 戊 the Yang Earth stem mow/wu. If you look closely, you will notice that mow lacks a horizontal stroke to the left. That is the only difference and indeed there is only a shade of difference between them in meaning. Both are Yang Earth. That is to say that they are big, solid and immoveable. Each signifies the qualities of loyalty and faith as well as stubbornness. Which of these is predominant is a question of balance; but we can immediately, as an example, divine something of the character of those born under mow sute/wu su 戊戌 the Earth Dog of 1958 and indeed 2018. Earth Dogs are often successful business women. Such a Dog may possess a near superhuman perseverance. They may equally not receive criticism well or adapt readily. It may well be that the double Earth of this Dog makes for a pillar sufficiently persistent to equip a woman to succeed in a man's world.

Interestingly the heraldic imagery of mediaeval Europe invested the Dog with the quality of loyalty. If the livery of a noble house depicted a Dog, it meant either that the family concerned considered itself a byword for loyalty or (more likely) demanded it. Similarly, a cloud meant the blessings of heaven which as we shall see, is very close to the Chinese idea of the Dragon. Similar correspondences appear in cultures all over the world.

Like the Dog, each animal has an elemental value:

## The Twelve Earthly Branches

| Rat | Ox | Tiger | Rabbit | Dragon | Snake |
|---|---|---|---|---|---|
| 子 | 丑 | 寅 | 卯 | 辰 | 巳 |
| chee | chou | yan | muw | shun | jee |
| tze | chou | yin | muw | zhen | si |
| water | earth | wood | wood | earth | fire |
| **Horse** | **Sheep** | **Monkey** | **Rooster** | **Dog** | **Pig** |
| 午 | 未 | 申 | 酉 | 戌 | 亥 |
| ng | may | shen | yuw | sute | hoi |
| wu | wei | shen | yuw | su | hai |
| fire | earth | metal | metal | earth | water |

Notice the very different distribution. As we noted earlier, there is an Earth character every three and the sequence opens with Water rather than Wood.

Fundamentally the order is actually the same: Water, Wood, Fire, Metal. It is simply that the four Earth animals are placed separately as punctuation rather than between Fire and Metal where they belong in the Cycle of Production.

Each Animal of course also has a polarity; that is, it is yin or yang.

### The Twelve Earthly Branches

The logic of the elemental qualities assigned to each animal becomes apparent when we notice the months and hours each represents. Fire, heat and rapid activity all fall logically towards the middle both of day and year just as cold and damp fall into the latter part.

| | | | | | |
|---|---|---|---|---|---|
| **Rat** | **Ox** | **Tiger** | **Rabbit** | **Dragon** | **Snake** |
| 子 | 丑 | 寅 | 卯 | 辰 | 巳 |
| chee | chou | yan | muw | shun | jee |
| tze | chou | yin | muw | zhen | si |
| water | earth | wood | wood | earth | fire |
| yang | yin | yang | yin | yang | yin |
| **Horse** | **Sheep** | **Monkey** | **Rooster** | **Dog** | **Pig** |
| 午 | 未 | 申 | 酉 | 戌 | 亥 |
| ng | may | shen | yuw | sute | hoi |
| wu | wei | shen | yuw | su | hai |
| fire | earth | metal | metal | earth | water |
| yang | yin | yang | yin | yang | yin |

**A Note About 24-Hour Clocks**: Chinese thinkers, who tended to think in terms of process as much as outcome, designed a clock with twelve double-hours.* Not only is this in some ways a better 24-hour clock than our own but it is also a demonstration of the priority of process over outcome. The middle of the day is not at noon but sometime between 11 a.m. and 1 p.m., during the hour of the Horse. The middle of the night similarly spans the double hour of the Rat, between 11 p.m. and 1 a.m.

*The earliest measurement may have divided 24 hours into 50 units. Unwieldy!

Notice now that the Rat is of the Water element and hence represents dead of night. Also notice that the Horse is Fire and sits at midday. After the Horse we will of course find first the punctuation of Earth (every third character) in the Sheep and then the Metal of the Monkey and Rooster (next in the Cycle of Production if the Earth is distributed differently). Observe how the logic of their distribution around the clock is inevitable. It could not be any other way. When is the hour of the Rabbit? Just after dawn, following the Tiger as you'd expect, when the Yin Wood shows itself as a fresh day.

**A Note About Maps**: We can incidentally, at this point note that the Chinese convention of placing South at the top both of maps and compass is actually the placing of the Fire element. Wherever we are, Northern or Southern Hemisphere, Pole or Tropic, the source of all Fire, that is to say the sun, is 93,000 million miles above us. There is no location on Earth where this does not hold. This suggests incidentally that technical arguments about reversing portents in the Southern Hemisphere may be barking up the wrong tree.

### The Twelve Earthly Branches with Hours

| **Rat** | **Ox** | **Tiger** | **Rabbit** | **Dragon** | **Snake** |
|---|---|---|---|---|---|
| 子 | 丑 | 寅 | 卯 | 辰 | 巳 |
| chee | chou | yan | muw | shun | jee |
| tze | chou | yin | muw | zhen | si |
| water | earth | wood | wood | earth | fire |
| 11-01 | 01-03 | 03-05 | 05-07 | 07-09 | 09-11 |

| **Horse** | **Sheep** | **Monkey** | **Rooster** | **Dog** | **Pig** |
|---|---|---|---|---|---|
| 午 | 未 | 申 | 酉 | 戌 | 亥 |
| ng | may | shen | yuw | sute | hoi |
| wu | wei | shen | yuw | su | hai |
| fire | earth | metal | metal | earth | water |
| 11-13 | 13-15 | 15-17 | 17-19 | 19-21 | 21-23 |

The months are completely consistent. The darkest month is December so obviously the Rat sits here as he does at midnight. The Rooster presides over early evening and therefore of course the autumn. Rooster's element is Metal which represents both the money counted up at the end of a day and the culmination of each growing season. Metal also connotes the mouth which may crow, sing or drink in celebration either of the safe storage of the harvest or the successful completion of another day.

## The Twelve Earthly Branches with Hours and Months

| Rat | Ox | Tiger | Rabbit | Dragon | Snake |
|---|---|---|---|---|---|
| 子 | 丑 | 寅 | 卯 | 辰 | 巳 |
| chee | chou | yan | muw | shun | jee |
| tze | chou | yin | muw | zhen | si |
| water | earth | wood | wood | earth | fire |
| 11-01 | 01-03 | 03-05 | 05-07 | 07-09 | 09-11 |
| Dec | Jan | Feb | Mar | April | May |

| Horse | Sheep | Monkey | Rooster | Dog | Pig |
|---|---|---|---|---|---|
| 午 | 未 | 申 | 酉 | 戌 | 亥 |
| ng | may | shen | yuw | sute | hoi |
| wu | wei | shen | yuw | su | hai |
| fire | earth | metal | metal | earth | water |
| 11-13 | 13-15 | 15-17 | 17-19 | 19-21 | 21-23 |
| June | July | Aug | Sep | Oct | Nov |

When we put stem and branch one on top of the other, we have the *Pillars*. Hence Four Pillars of Destiny, consisting of eight images – or *Ba Zi*. There are Twelve Animals and Five Elements, hence 60 Pillars. This is the *gan zi* Cycle, the Cycle of Time and Space.

**Some Notes About Which Year Which Animal Falls Into**: There are twelve Zodiac Animals and twelve months in the Gregorian (i.e. Western) calendar. So the Ox always falls in January (usually starting around the 6th); the Tiger always in February (usually the 4th); the Dragon in April (usually the 5th) and so on. Easy to master.

**There are also twelve double hours in the Chinese day**. So 11 a.m. to 1 p.m. is always the Horse Hour, followed by the Sheep and so on. Again easy. Days are more tricky but the Years even easier if you've followed the logic.

**There are ten Stems and ten integers** (the numbers 0–9) and a year ending in zero always has a Yang Metal Stem, a year ending in one having a Yin Metal stem and so on.

Hence 2024 is a Yang Wood Dragon year and 2025 a Wood Snake Year. Working back from that. 2012 is a Water Dragon year and 2013 a Water Snake. If you can just subtract twelve it gets very easy indeed. And in fact the simple exercise of subtracting sixty will allow you to locate the Pillar of any year past or future. To get even more ambitious if 2026 was a Fire Horse, then so was 1966, but also 1666 and 1726. Examination of these correspondences can be very revealing and many feng shui masters (including myself) do just that annually before attempting to forecast what the next coming year may hold.

## What Next?

Next we draft the Ba Zi. Typically, this is between two and four hours of work. You will notice that I emphasise stopping regularly to interpret as you go along.

I would actually suggest that before you start you get centred, sit quietly, breathe into yourself and *feel*. Aim from this moment on to be aware of every hint the universe may be offering you: your own feelings, noises off, music on the edge of your attention, writing that catches your eye, your mood and the events of the day. Above all seek *qing* – the quality of caring. Nothing changes unless somebody gives a damn. Emotive music may help.

In the modules that follow we will introduce, explain and elaborate upon the various aspects of the Ba Zi (principally *sap sans,* rules for combination and clash as well as *san sats* (i.e. special stars and Palaces) that make it such a three-dimensional assessment of a person's prospects.

Watch this space…

**A Note About the Beginning of Solar Months**: The Chinese Months we are dealing with are Solar and approximate (but only approximate) to Months in the Gregorian (i.e. Western) Calendar. The Ox Month is almost the same as January but usually starts around 6 January. The dates at the top of the columns of the Chinese Calendar mark New Moons that is to say Lunar Months which is useful information you'll need later but is peripheral for now.

**A Note About Solar and Lunar Months**: Jack Chiu's Calendar and many fully Chinese Calendars highlight the beginning of the Solar Month in bold, in Jack's case bold pink. It is this date that opens our Chinese Solar Month. So for instance on page 371 the Ox Month (which you can recognise because of the Ox character (丑) on the second row from the top of that column begins on the $5^{th}$, the Tiger Month (February) on the $6^{th}$ and so on).

The Calendar may look daunting but essentially it is just the Gregorian, Lunar and Solar Calendars superimposed on the Gan Zhi Cycle. Complex is just lots of simple. Honest.

See Calendar on pp. 197–8.

**A Note About Becoming Centred**: One powerful method of self-centring is a Sufi procedure I learned from Andrew Harvey. It consists of repeating the words "La Illaha Il Allah, La Illaha Il Allah" (Everything is God) until in the way of such repetition you are pretty much out of your mind. Ask the nearest tree why it is there or allow the sky to tell you what it knows. Then return to the Ba Zi.

# Constructing the Four Pillars of Destiny

## Drafting the *Ba Zi* with Richard Ashworth

### Stage 1: Reading from the 10,000 Year Calendar

| **Noon**<br>**Hour** | **16th**<br>**Day** | **October**<br>**Month** | **2023**<br>**Year** |
|---|---|---|---|
| Fire<br>丙 | Fire<br>丁 | Water<br>壬 | Water<br>癸 |
| Horse<br>午 | Sheep<br>未 | Dog<br>戌 | Rabbit<br>卯 |

**Hint**: *Add provisional interpretation as you go along. Any number of things that occur to you may prove relevant.*

1. Write **Name and Birth details** in the correct space on the form. (**In Table above, see p. 211.**)
   **Interpret.** There may be something in the name or your experience worth noting.

2. Write (*as much as possible from memory*).

**2023**
**Year**
癸
Rabbit
卯

**The Year Pillar** (i.e. its Stem and Branch) is on the Year Page in the Chinese 10,000 Year Calendar. Usually about two-thirds down the right-hand page.
See p. 225: you'll find the Year 2023 (illustrated) top left of page 368 of Jack Chiu's English translation* next to the

* Available from Jack at **jack.chiu@acmc.com.hk** reproduced with his permission. There are other calendars which you may come across which are a little harder to apply and indeed to find. I usually have a stock and offer one-to-one tuition online when appropriate.

Chinese characters gui 癸 and Muw 卯 which form the Water Rabbit Pillar of 2023 thus: 癸

卯

**Interpret.** What do you know, think or feel about Rabbits or Water?

3. Write (*as much as possible from memory*).

**October**

**<u>Month</u>**

Water

壬

Dog

戌

**The Month Pillar characters** are on the second row down of each of the twelve month columns. Above them are characters indicating whether the month is for notation purposes a long or short one. In practice all you need do is look at the foot of each column to identify whether it is short or long; a long one has 30 days, a short one 29 (see pp. 225–26).

Under the Month Stem and Branch characters is the *gua* or *lo shu* number of the month. Jack Chiu expresses it as an Arabic (that is Western) numeral.

The Water 壬 Dog 戌 Month October 2023 is a short Month with an 8 gua.

**Interpret:** what occurs to you? How do you feel? How might this apply?

(If the Day falls between the 4th and the 9th approach with caution. Find the start of the Chinese month (which in Jack Chiu's calendar is highlighted) and work from there. This Dog Month, as you can see, opens on October 8 (10/8), the subsequent Pig Month on November 8 (11/8). So the 16th is emphatically in the Dog Month.)

4. Write (*from calendar page*).

**16th**
**Day**
Fire
丁
Sheep
未

**The Pillar of the Day** we are working on, 16 October (10/16) is: 丁 未

The Branch (i.e. Animal) at the top of the Month Column can often mislead. Be led by the highlighted date. February 4 for instance almost always opens the Tiger Month regardless of the column it falls into and very often (as in 2023) appears on the previous page. The first date 1/22 (January 22) always listed at the top left of the page is the New Moon which marks the Lunar New Year.

5. Write (*from calendar page*).

**16th**
**Hour**
Fire
丙
Horse
午

**The Pillar of the Hour** we are working on, midday on the 16 October (10/16) is: 丙 午

**The Hour Pillar** consists of the Hour Branch – which you'll know how to assess by now – plus a Stem. Noon of course falls into the Horse Double Hour. The Stem is found by looking at the table known as the **Five Rats** which you'll find on page 419 of Jack's Almanac. **You'll also find this table on p. 224, at the end of this book.**

On that table we look for the Day Stem at the top of one of the columns. The Stem of the 17 October 2023 is ding 丁 as we saw above which is in a box with Ren 壬 second from the right. Follow your finger down to *Wu* the Horse (午), the Hour Branch we're working with, and note the Stem. That Stem is bing 丙. So the Hour Pillar is: 丙
午

We take the hour at face value wherever birth took place as you know, unless it's been distorted by human interference such as Daylight Savings Time.

**So the Four Pillars are:**

| **Noon**<br>**Hour** | **16th**<br>**Day** | **October**<br>**Month** | **2023**<br>**Year** |
|---|---|---|---|
| Fire | Fire | Water | Water |
| 丙 | 丁 | 癸 | 癸 |
| Horse | Sheep | Dog | Rabbit |
| 午 | 未 | 戌 | 卯 |

6. **Calculate Life House**:

| **Life House** |
|---|
| Wood |
| 乙 |
| Ox |
| 丑 |

1. Consult Calendar for whether the day is in the first or second Solar Fortnight.

   If in the second fortnight it belongs to the following month *for this purpose only.*

   Jack prints the mid-point of the Month in red. The first Solar Fortnight of October 2023, as you can see ends on the 24th i.e. 10/24. The precise hour of that change 0:21 is listed above the column of dates. The upper hour relates to the upper (lightly) highlighted date and the lower to the lower (boldly highlighted) which marks the beginning of the following (Pig) month on 8 November (8/11). The number printed next to these times refers to where the corresponding Solar Fortnight falls in the sequence of twenty-four Solar fortnights. We will address this later.
2. Consult *Life House Branch Finder* table (p. 217) to tie corrected (Zodiac) Month Animal to Hour Branch on grid to show Life House Branch (i.e. Animal).
3. Consult *5 Tigers chasing* table (page 415 in Jack's Almanac, also, on p. 223, at the end of this book), tying up Year Stem (here *quai* yin Water 癸) with the Life House Branch (in this case Ox 丑) on p. 189 to identify Life House stem – in this case Yi 乙.

So now we have a Life House:

| Life House | Noon Hour | 16th Day | October Month | 2023 Year |
|---|---|---|---|---|
| Wood | Fire | Fire | Water | Water |
| 乙 | 丙 | 丁 | 癸 | 癸 |
| Ox | Horse | Sheep | Dog | Rabbit |
| 丑 | 午 | 未 | 戌 | 卯 |

**Interpret**: if this Pillar were talking to the rest of the Ba Zi what would it be saying?

**A Note About the Life House**: Master Chan Kun Wah with whom I studied pretty much full time for several years, used to say that if the subject is a car, then the Life House is its garage. For myself, more than twenty years and thousands of Ba Zis later, I'd add that the Life House may equally be the voice that calls to us. Each Pillar not only occupies a Year, Month etc., but has a particular nature. That nature may represent an aspiration, frustration or calling. It is the subject's business how they respond to it but broadly the call wants embracing or rejecting and which it is may be a chronic puzzle.

## 7. Calculate Big Fate/Luck Pillars

1. Ascertain the direction the Big Fate progresses from the Month Pillar: yang (that is forward) for male born in even year and yang for female born in odd year. Yin motion otherwise. The first Big Fate Pillar will always be either the next pillar forward in the *gan zi* cycle from the Month Pillar or the next one back.

2. Calculate the starting point from the calendar page: If yang motion, move forward to the start of the next Chinese month, yin back to start of current month. 3 days = 1 year (i.e. 1 day = 4 months)
3. If it moves forward (yang) put next Stem and Branch in the *gan zi* cycle from month pillar into the boxes.
4. Fill in 5 and 10-year anniversaries of change of Big Fate. Note the most current date.
5. Fill in years plus stem and branch from start year.

**Interpret:**

**A Note About the Big Fate**: The Pillars of the Big Fate follow the gan zi Cycle and change every 10 years. They start with the Pillar immediately after (Yang i.e. forwards motion) or before (Yin i.e. backwards) the subject's Month Pillar depending on whether they are respectively either male in an even numbered year/female in an odd numbered year or the other way round.

Each 10-Year progression can bring a very different ambient qi.

**A Note About the Big Fate or "Luck" Pillars**: The Big Fate can kick in any time from the day of birth to late in the tenth year of life. Which can indicate respectively, birth trauma or early separation from Mother and a sheltered upbringing or a very profound inner life. It often (but not always) accompanies trauma, invariably a psychologically important event. Examples include parental separation, illness, accident, reversal of fortune and birth of a sibling. My own Big Fate kicks in at 1 Year 4 Months and as it happens, I have twin sisters almost precisely 1 Year 4 Months younger than me.

Don't be too concerned to identify the very moment. The Big Fate represents a decision made by a child about life, and decisions may precede a critical event or follow it. Equally we may not remember a very early Big Fate event. But it'll be there. And, of course, the ambience created changes with each fresh Big Fate Pillar every ten years or so. If the change it brings is not noticeable at 6, it may be at 16 or 26.

8. Enter **Hidden Stems** from table on p. 218.

**A Note About Hidden Stems**: The Hidden stems remind us that the Ba Zi is essentially made up of Stems. This is if you like, the molecular theory of Ba Zi. I recommend careful study of the Hidden Stems table because it illustrates so clearly that Ba Zi is like feng shui, all about patterns. Hidden Stems can also tell us about the fine tuning of a Ba Zi: someone born say in the Yang Metal part of a Snake Hour may be quite different from someone with an otherwise identical Ba Zi. Some Masters can tell how many children the subject may have and indeed their genders. And much more from the Hidden Stems alone.

Now we add detail:

1. ***Kua*** number and group (calculate using formula below) **(See Cycle of Change forms on pp. 213–216)**

   **Here's the calculation:**

   1. Add up all the digits of the year. e.g. 1+9+5+7=22
   2. Keep adding until you end up with a single digit. e.g. 2+2=4
   3. **For Men:** Subtract from 11 (treat 10 as 1) e.g 11-4=7

**For Women:** add to 4 e.g. 4+4=8
If the result is 5:
**Man:** 2
**Woman:** 8.
**Interpret.** Numbers have meanings.

**A Note About Kua Numbers:** Notice the differing calculations for the genders which is not reflected in the calculation of what is known as *9 Star Ki*. A 9 Star Ki Master can often tell extraordinary things from just three numbers. Chinese Masters, however, tend to discount this (Japanese) method. Diviners vary as to how much info they need, of course.

**Caution:** if you're looking at dates far into the past (or future) don't trust the kuas printed in the (green print) Cycles of Change graphic which are accurate only for the current cycle of 60 years.

**Interpret:** do these numbers mean anything to you?

2. ***Lap yum* (see Cycles of Change table pp. 213–16)**

**A Note About *Lap Yums*:** Again, not strictly a Ba Zi calculation (they are actually a ring on the luo pan) but there is a brief description of their meaning in the (green print) Cycles of Change graphic which may be helpful. If you have a feel for Chinese numerology they can be very useful. You might experiment with calculating lap yums for the Day and Month which can often be more readily apposite.

**Interpret:** consider the brief note about lap yums in the context of this Ba Zi.

3. *Xuang kong da gua* (from Cycles of Change table pp. 213–216)

**A Note About *Xuan Kong Da Gua*:** Again not strictly a Ba Zi calculation but if you have a feel for Chinese numerology they can be very useful. And they will come in handy when you are matching feng shui procedures to a Ba Zi. XKDG by the way is a very big topic and this application to Ba Zi barely touches the surface.

**Interpret**: how do these two numbers interact?

4. **Animal Nature** (from Cycles of Change table pp. 213–16)

**A Note About Animal Natures**: And also not a Ba Zi calculation but can be quite informative. More in Kwok Man Ho's *Authentic Chinese Horoscopes* if you want to explore this.

**Interpret**

Interpret: how do the Hidden Stems alter the apparent balance of the Ba Zi?

5. Enter **Sap Sans** from table (special care with Life House and Day Pillar) on pp. 193, 221 & 116–131.

**Note:** The polarity of Water and Fire branches (Pig, Rat, Horse, Snake) are reversed for Sap San calculation.

Interpret Ba Zi to date and pay special attention to Day and Life House Pillars.

**A Note About Correspondences between Chinese and Western Zodiacs**: the second Solar fortnight of each Chinese Solar Month opens precisely when the Western Zodiac Animal changes: in this case on 24 October from Libra to Scorpio. This and the recurrence of cycles of 60 and 30 both here and in the Western calendar and clock suggest common ancestors, possibly in Cimmerian or Babylonian systems.

## Stage 2: Adding Interpretative Detail (and Colour)

1. Annotate the **8-year cycle** **Red**
   Interpret

**A Note About the Eight Year Cycle**: the tradition is that the first eight years of life are under the influence of the Year Stem (i.e. same-gender parent); the next eight under the influence of the Year Branch (i.e. opposite gender parent); the next eight the Month Stem and so on. Following that pattern will find you writing 56 by the Hour Stem and 64 by the Hour Branch. This is orthodox. I usually add 72 and 80 to the Life House Stem and Branch respectively. Which is not so orthodox.

2. Mark **now** (appropriate Pillar) and **self** (on Day Stem), **Red**
   see pp. 138–180
   Interpret
3. Mark **Combinations, Clashes, Triggers**, see pp. 138–180 **Red**
   Interpret
4. Mark in **Hidden Stem** positions, see p. 218 **Red**
   Interpret
5. Plot **Palaces** from table on p. 219
   (Pay attention to Life House and Day Pillar) **Green**
   Interpret
6. Plot **Empty Palaces** (note meaning), see p. 220 **Green**
   Interpret

**A Note About Interpretative Detail:** the suggested colours may ease interpretation.

**Annotating the 8-year cycle** follows the tradition that years 1–8 relate to the same-gender parent in some way, the next the opposite gender parent and so on. Mapped onto the Big Fate this can offer nuance to a Big Fate Pillar.

**Marking** ***now*** **(appropriate Pillar) and** ***self*** **(on Day Stem)** lets you know much about the subject's current situation.

Interpret

**Marking Combinations, Clashes, Triggers** adds nuance as well as allowing adjustment to the strength or weakness of a Ba Zi.

**Marking in Hidden Stem positions**: To assess how they may affect interpretation of the relative Pillar.

**Plotting Palaces from table**: (Pay attention to Life House and Day Pillar) lets you assess the health, maturity and stage in life of the subject regardless of age or Elemental balance.

**Plotting Empty Palaces (note meaning on pp. 192 & 220)** can reveal ambiguity or emphasis. An Empty Pillar containing good portents may be compromised and vice versa.

## Stage 3: Strength and Timing

1. **Calculate strength** (and thus completing element):
2. **Assess Timing**: is day stem in a supportive season?
3. **Assess Support**, e.g., yan and bay gin? (too much™ = strong)

   How much kun and sik sun (too much = weak)
   Bear in mind Combinations and **Triggers**

   **Interpret**

4. Add in **San Sats** i.e. Special Stars, pp. 180–205

   e.g. What's missing? What's needed?

   **Interpret**

**A Note About Strength and Weakness**: A "strong" Ba Zi (that is Day Stem) is not "good" any more than a "weak" one is "bad"; they're all unbalanced. Which is not necessarily a disadvantage. Knowing the strength of a Ba Zi, however, does allow us to consider what intervention may serve them best. A balanced Ba Zi by the way is in my observation more affected by outside influences such as the change of year, Fate Pillar or location.

**A Note About Psychic Protection**: some practitioners, realising how much emotional and other transference there can be between subject and practitioner, prepare with some method of psychic protection. The brilliant William Bloom has for instance published at least one book on this topic and indeed has taught Psychic Protection Workshops. For myself, I don't do it. I am pretty sure that the ability to get "under the skin" of a Ba Zi is related to being prepared to feel the feelings, good, bad or ugly of the subject. I routinely carry away with me the pain of someone I have been working with and if I armour myself against it, I may not ever really get what's going on. You may or may not want to take this advice. Your call.

## Reference Material

**10,000 Year Calendar**

such as:

Hong Kong: 962-8123-77-7

Joey Yap: (this is in English). 983-40761-5-0

Jack Chiu: (this is part English/part Chinese) 978-988188462-6

(The calendar includes Rats and Tigers *Chasing* tables)

Plus:

Stephanie Stewart 978-0-578-32792-1

A Student's Key to the Hsia Calendar

Best to order direct from Stephanie: seriousfengshui@gmail.com

**Included in this book:**

**Tables***:*

1. Ba Zi drafting form (two sheets), pp. 211–12
2. Cycles of Change table, pp. 213–16, which includes:

   *Kua* Numbers
   *Lap Yums*
   *Xuan Kong Da Guas*
   Animal Nature

3. Life House Branch (ie Animal) Finder, p. 217
4. Hidden Stems Table, p. 218
5. Palaces Table, p. 219
6. Empty Palaces Table, p. 220
7. Sap Sans, p. 221
8. Solar Fortnights, p. 222
9. Five Tigers Chasing, p. 223
10. Five Rats Chasing, p. 224

**A Note About Drafting from Memory**: First master the fact that the Branches (that is Animals) fall tidily into the 12 Month and 12 Double-Hour Cycle while the Stems fall into the 10 Integer pattern. Then we can get a bit cleverer.

**Writing the Year Stem and Branch from memory** is very simple. Take say, 1989. We know 2024 has been a Wood Dragon Year and so 12 years before, 2012 was a Water Dragon. Give this a moment's thought perhaps. The Stems run through the Cycle of Production (Yang Water, Yin Water-Yang Wood, Yin Wood-Yang Fire, Yin Fire-Yang Earth, Yin Earth-Yang Metal, Yin Metal) so the Dragon Year previous to a Wood Dragon will be a Water Dragon. By the same token, previous to that Water Dragon was the Metal Dragon of 2000; 12 years before that an Earth Dragon in 1988. So 1989 there is going to be an Earth Snake. Simples.

Over time you may simply apply multiples of 60 to identify the Pillar of any year ever. 1689? Also an Earth Snake. 1712: Water Dragon. And so on.

**What about the Month Stem**? Here's the thing: since the Gan Zi Cycle of Stems and Branches is 60 Pillars long, it repeats every 60 years but also every 60 Months, every 60 Days and every 60 Hours. 60 Months is precisely 5 years. So if you know that the Stem of the Horse Month of say 2022 is Yang Fire, you know the same is true also of 2027 and 2032. Equally simples. Watch this space for the Hour Stem. You can always, of course, just consult the Chinese Calendar.

## A Note About Sap Sans*

1. Knowing the cycle (earth>metal>water>wood>fire>earth) of production and (earth>water>fire>metal>wood>earth) destruction is essential in order to understand this.
2. The sap sans are a way of expressing the relationship between the day stem and the other characters in the Ba Zi. They express what each element means to the day stem within the particular Ba Zi as well as its more universal meaning. There are Five Elements and therefore Five Relationships, two polarities hence ten variations.
3. These relationships are:

| | | |
|---|---|---|
| Bay gin | *friends* | i.e. the same element as the day stem. |
| Sik sun | *expression* | the element produced by the day stem. |
| Choi | *prizes* | element destroyed/controlled by the day stem. |
| Kun | *challenge* | the element that destroys/controls the day stem. |
| Yan | *resource* | the element that produces the day stem. |

3. Each has a same and a reverse polarity expression.

Bay gin is the same polarity as the day stem; its counterpart is called gip choi which means "rob wealth".

Sik sun is also the same polarity; its counterpart is zeun kun which means something like "steal power".

Choi can be opposite polarity (jing choi – fair reward) or the same polarity (pin choi) which means "indirect reward".

Kun can be jing (fair challenge) or pin: "unwarranted" or "harsh".

Yan can be jing (attentive parent) or pin: "accidental" or "indirect".

4. For bay gin and sik sun, same polarity is broadly "good" and reverse broadly "bad". For choi, kun and yan, reverse polarity is broadly "good" and same polarity broadly "bad".
5. For the purposes of sap san calculation, polarity of Fire and Water branches reverses i.e. Snake and Pig yang and Rat and Horse yin.

*This is actually a sneak preview of Module II.

**A Note About Strength and Weakness**

A weak Ba Zi is not bad any more than a strong one is good; they're both unbalanced, as are most Ba Zis to a greater or lesser extent. Actually, a balanced one is particularly hard to work with. What we're aiming to do with a Ba Zi is to help a person make use of opportunity.

We all pretty much want success, creativity and influence. That is to say: *choi, sik sun/zeun kun* and *kun*. To this end we will boost a weak Ba Zi so that the person is up to pursuing such opportunities and we'll challenge a strong one to make use of their advantage.

What makes a Ba Zi strong or weak?

Views differ but the consensus appears to be that *timeliness* is central. Timeliness is simply the degree to which the Day Stem has fallen into a season that supports it. For example, a *gap/chia* 甲 Day Stem being Yang Wood, is supported by Water and Wood. Hence a gap/chia 甲

Day Stem born in winter (the Water season) or spring (the Wood season) is timely and therefore well supported and likely to be considered strong.

A similar Ba Zi with a gap/chia 甲 Day Stem but born in summer or autumn would generally be considered weak. Sometimes an inspection of the precise Hidden Stem that the birth date falls upon in the Month Pillar can be an important additional detail.

Most Masters factor in the support of other Stems and Branches in the Ba Zi in a similar way. So, a gap/chia 甲 Day Stem with Rabbits, Tigers, Rats and Pigs and/or Water and Wood stems would have additional strength.

Many would also consider combinations that bolster the Day Stem as strengthening. In this case the Ba Zi would be made stronger by combinations to Water and Wood. Some may only be potential.

We will assess these factors as we decide on Elements that may help:

**A strong Ba Zi** broadly wants to be challenged.
This means it needs *choi, sik sun/zeun kun* and/or *kun*.

**A weak Ba Zi** wants to be bolstered.
This means it needs *bay gin/gip choi* and *yan*.

There are other types of imbalance, such as hot/cold, wet/dry and so on as well as *special forms* but these are beyond the remit of this starter course.

# Module II: The Ba Zi Toolbox

What Chinese Masters have constantly attempted over the years is to précis complex information into a single, pithy image. Into this category fall the Sap Sans or *10 Gods*, the lap yums and fin kams (or *pieces of gold*) and the fraction-like kuas drawn from Xuan Kong Da Gua feng shui. Each of these devices goes some way towards distilling a complex relationship down to a single idea that can be worked with easily. In the case of sap sans, this relationship is that between the Day Stem and each of the Five Elements. The Day stem of course is the reference point of the Ba Zi. Sap Sans allow us to tell what each Element means in relation to a particular Ba Zi.

## 1. The Sap Sans or Elementals

Masters sometimes call the Sap Sans the *10 Gods, Useful Gods* or *10 Fairies*. Like many such translations into English, these terms carry a certain amount of unfortunate luggage; *Elementals* might be a better rendering, as what these characters stand for is precisely the elemental relationship between the Day Stem (or Day Master) and the rest of the characters as those relationships appear in a particular, individual Ba Zi. This relationship depends obviously enough both on the element of the Day Stem and its polarity. So, another benefit of this shorthand is that it makes quite clear the difference between the behaviour of yin and yang stems.

So, although Metal may generally be considered symbolic of something like precision, accuracy or competition, and Fire something like discovery; for say, a Wood Day Stem, each of these elements takes on some very different and additional shades of meaning. In such a case any Metal clashes the Wood of the Stem which means that Metal in relation to Wood takes on the sap san *kun* – that is challenge, discipline or influence. Fire on the other hand, is produced by Wood, and hence is *sik sun* or *output* to a Wood-day stem. So, in such a case Metal becomes the challenge of precision and Fire the purpose of curiosity. A Ba Zi containing these conjunctions might in some circumstances belong to an inventor or at least a creative thinker.

Equally the sap sans derived from the Yang Wood stem *jia/gap* 甲 are very different to those derived from the Yin Wood stem yi/*yute* 乙.

The sap sans allow us to draw some far-reaching conclusions about meaning within a Ba Zi.

To explain how this is so, we have to an extent to return to First Principles.

## The Cycle of Production or Creation

A simple way to master this is to see it as a clock.

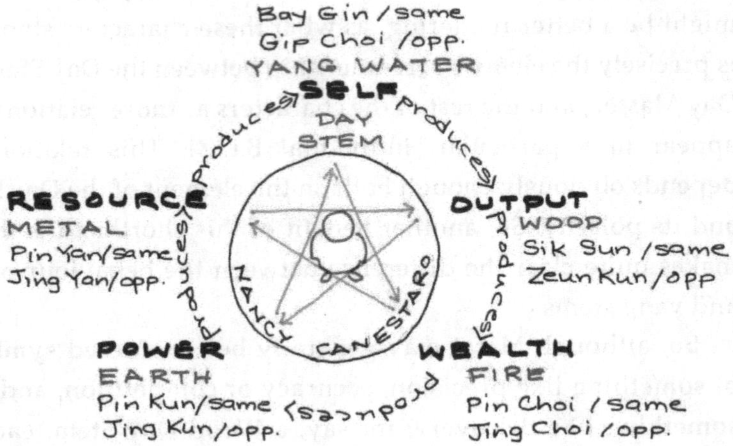


DAY STEM 壬 REN, YANG WATER

**SAP SANS / TEN GODS**

| | LIFE HOUSE | TIME | DAY | MONTH | YEAR |
|---|---|---|---|---|---|
| POLARITY | YIN | YANG | YANG | YANG | YIN |
| 5-ELEM. | EARTH | FIRE | WATER | WATER | FIRE |
| STEM | 己 | 丙 | 壬 | 壬 | 丁 |
| STEM | JI | BING | REN | REN | DING |
| ANIMAL | ROOSTER | HORSE | DOG | TIGER | PIG |
| BRANCH | YOU | WU | XU | YIN | HAI |
| BRANCH | 酉 | 午 | 戌 | 寅 | 亥 |
| 5-ELEM. | METAL | FIRE | EARTH | WOOD | WATER |
| POLARITY | YIN | YANG | YANG | YANG | YIN |

**The Cycle of Production or Creation with Sap Sans**

## The Sap Sans of the Wood Day Stem

**Wood** produces **Fire**; so, fire is the sap san sik sun, that is the *output, creativity* or *intelligence* of wood. Fire is the *work* or *occupation* of wood; some might say it is the *meaning* of wood.
**Fire** retains its own qualities while it gains these further overtones.

**Wood** crushes **Earth**; so, Earth is the sap san choi, that is the *wealth, success, prey* or *conquest* of wood. Earth is the *possession* or *trophy* of wood; some might say it is the *reward* of wood.
**Earth** retains its own qualities while it gains these further overtones.

**Wood** is crushed by **Metal**; so, Metal is the sap san kun, that is the *power, discipline, influence* or *challenge* of wood. Metal is the *authority* or *adversary* of wood; some might say the *conqueror* of wood.
**Metal** retains its own qualities while it gains these further overtones.

**Wood** is produced by **Water**; so, Water is the sap san yan, that is the *parent, resource* or *supporter* of wood. Water is the *home* or *family* of wood; some might say it is the *womb* of wood.
**Water** retains its own qualities while it gains these further overtones.

**Wood** is itself **Wood**; so, wood is the sap san bay gin, that is the *peer, sibling* or *team mate* of wood. Wood is the *friend* or *brother* of wood; some might say it is the *self* of wood.
**Wood** retains its own qualities while it gains these further overtones.

This pattern is true of each of the elements: the element that is produced by the Day Stem is sik sun/zeun kun or Output, that which is controlled or clashed by the Day Stem is choi or Wealth, that which controls or clashes the Day Stem is kun or Challenge, that which produces the Day Stem is yan (Resources), that which is the same element as the Day Stem is bay gin/gip choi (Self).

## Jing and Pin, the Polarity of the Sap Sans

In common with all aspects of feng shui and Ba Zi, an understanding of the polarity, that is the (something like) gender of the sap sans is crucial. In point of fact in certain circumstances, a yin sap san can have a very different meaning to its yang counterpart. This is highly nuanced information, however, and should not be seen as cast in stone. We always retain free will and from my standpoint (you don't have to agree), everything is a function of choice.

Like most symbolic information, a sap san will suggest a tendency, not necessarily an inevitability. I am often astonished by the ability of a person with a challenging Ba Zi to behave in a way that draws the very best from the cards dealt them.

## A Note About Jing and Pin

You will have noticed that three of the sap sans come in recognisable pairs – *jing* and *pin*. Jing is the opposite polarity and pin the same polarity. Broadly (careful with this) jing is the good guy and pin the opposite.

In the "Output" (sik sun/zeun kun) and "Self" (bay gin/gip choi) pairs, the first of these is same polarity. And the dynamic is the opposite; broadly same polarity is the good guy. All of these are subject to context, nuance and judgement call, of course.

One application for instance of sap sans is to identify members of the family within the Ba Zi. Mother is yan, the resource. Wood is yan to Fire because Wood gives birth to it. The rules for this are straightforward, as we shall see and integrally connected to the fact that for each sap san there are two characters: one per polarity, each with an individual implication.

**A Note About Family:** A traditional marriage is a kun/choi relationship. This unreconstructed model perpetuates the role of woman as choi, that is prize or treasure and the man as lord, authority or conqueror. If we can for now overlook the potentially offensive patriarchal implications, we can observe that it is at least traditional that men can often on some level at least think of their relationship as a win and their partner as a prize or reward. Someone observed that if the (Men's) rugby team wins 50-0, the wives can expect a busy Saturday night.

Be that as it may, anyone's Mother is represented by the Element that produces them. In other words, for the purposes of family arrangement the Mother of a man with a chia 甲 Yang Wood Day stem is considered to be Yin Water (i.e. Yan or Resource, the Element that produced him and opposite polarity) and his Father Yang Earth i.e. the Element that clashes her and therefore choi (that is prize) to his son. These Elemental values may not equate to the actual Ba Zis concerned but they can tell us a great deal about family relationships.

**Important Note**: for sap san purposes, the Fire and Water Branches reverse their polarity. In other words, Rat and Horse are yin and Pig and Snake are yang. Note also that a sap san probably carries negative associations if it is either over- or under-represented. How it clashes or combines gives us more information again.

### A. Sik Sun *(same polarity) Direct Output and* Zeun Kun *Indirect Output (opposite polarity): Output, work, purpose, creativity, children*

Bay gin (self) produces sik sun.

Sik sun represents the Element produced by the Day Stem, sometimes termed *output.* The character sik sun actually means output of the same polarity, its counterpart zeun kun signifies output of the opposite polarity. These meanings can be very different. Sik sun is generally thought of as a more healthy, clean type of output while zeun kun is reckoned to be less so.

Some Masters call sik sun *Eating God,* an image that implies what is favoured or what demands attention. This interpretation is quite subtle and not necessarily entirely positive. Sometimes sik sun for instance, suggests a favourite or someone pampered. What both sik sun and zeun kun represent, however, is creativity, work and purpose.

Some Masters say that sik sun and zeun kun both represent children. This is something to be very careful with; it is generally true for a woman but often not for a man.* In point of fact, technically a man's children are kun, that is a *challenge* to him. It is usually accurate, however, to read the appearance of sik sun in a female Ba Zi as a choice between various forms of creativity including childbirth. Often a woman may for largely biological reasons, be torn between career and reproduction in a way a man generally is not. Sik sun represents the focus of our life which often (but not necessarily or always) means work for a man and children for a woman.

For either gender, sik sun can be creative intelligence, implying one who will never go hungry or lack opportunities. On the other hand, excess sik sun can imply excess independence leading to loneliness or the tendency to be misunderstood. It

---

* That sik sun is daughter, zeun kun son is to be approached with caution too.

can also accompany elegance. In the family, sik sun is a man's son-in-law.

Zeun kun on the other hand, is sometimes called *Hurting Officer* which generally connotes that which is neglected or needy, by extension the resentful. By further extension, it can signify the wrong path or an inappropriate career. Some Masters actually equate zeun kun with a life of forgery and plagiarism, even crime. Some Masters also equate it with, for a woman, multiple liaisons. In the family zeun kun is a man's mother-in-law and grandmother (via same-gender parent). By implication, zeun kun keeps women at a distance.

**A Note About Gods and Officers**: the Ba Zi model conceals a multitude of deep psychological, societal and other truths. And Hurting Officer and Eating God are very strange terms which contain an uncomfortable dichotomy: that a child is either spoiled or neglected. This may or may not be a valid duality but it certainly represents the fear of the concerned parent: is it inevitable that my child falls into one or other of these categories?

## *B.* Jing Choi *(Opposite Polarity) Direct Wealth and Pin Choi Indirect Wealth (Same Polarity): Wealth, Success, Achievement, Wife*

Sik sun produces choi.

Choi is what the day stem controls and is often thought of as success or wealth. The "choi" in the New Year greeting "gung hei fat choi" is this character. Choi is good to find in the Year Pillar where it implies a comfortable and safe upbringing because of course the Year Pillar represents parents, grandparents and family history as well as the years of childhood. Time moves from right to left in a Ba Zi.

Jing choi (the opposite polarity to the Day Stem) is *Direct Wealth* or Achievement. This is success, fairly won through effort and application. Jing choi is wife to a man (though not the converse). Wife in the unreconstructed Confucian view is possession, treasure, pearl. Husband (sap san jing kun) is lord, master, conqueror. Interestingly, a woman's father is also jing choi, that is, success that has been earned.

Often of course a man is a soft touch to his daughters but equally her relationship with her father is, like it or not, so often the source of a woman's power. My fieldwork suggests that the more powerful a woman, the more true this is. History is littered with evidence – Margaret Thatcher, Ghislaine Maxwell, Elizabeth I and Norah Jones are examples.

If there is no choi in a man's Ba Zi he may not find his perfect partner readily. Missing choi for either gender suggests lack of success though certain strong choi-free Ba Zis are able to exploit choi. In fact, a strong yang Day Stem can capitalise on pin choi because it is also yang and therefore among other things *bigger* than its yin equivalent. Strong yin Day Stems are thought to profit through effort but not win the Lottery! So jing choi implies a hardworking person who gives value for money. Unbalanced or poorly placed it can mean inconsistency.

Pin choi (same polarity) is *Indirect Wealth,* random rewards and wealth obtained by sheer luck, ill-gotten gains; and for a man – mistress. This quality is also equated with a suitability to be self-employed and indeed an incapacity to be employed. A person with disproportionate pin choi (as a rule of thumb, upwards of three characters) may have a weak work ethic; fecklessness and irresponsibility are often associated. In the family pin choi is a man's father. This seemingly perverse association may like so much sap san theory, allude to psychological if not literal truths. For a man, jing choi in the Day Branch means finding true love later rather than sooner. Perhaps pin choi is a father's unconditional love?

## *C. Jing Kun (Opposite Polarity) Direct Officer and Pin Kun (Same Polarity) Seven Killings: Power, Challenge, Authority, Discipline, Influence*

Choi produces kun.

*Kun* is challenge or discipline, the element that clashes or *controls* the Day Stem. Nothing, you will recall, happens without a clash, so to think of kun as purely negative of course, misses the point.

Whether a Ba Zi is looking for kun and choi for balance or bay gin and yan for support, depends essentially on its strength or weakness. We bolster a weak Ba Zi with bay gin and yan so as to make use of success and expression. Conversely, we drain a strong Day Stem so as to make use of them; not that weak is bad or strong good but to a strong Ba Zi, kun is healthy and to a weak one broadly not. Challenge and discipline to a strong Day Stem lead to influence. For a weak one, challenge may be too much without approval (bay gin) or support (yan).

Just as wife is jing choi to husband so husband is jing kun (opposite polarity) to wife and although children are sik sun (or creativity) to a woman, they are kun to a man (because she is choi which produces kun). A woman may be depleted (as a Day Stem is by sik sun) by the output of childbirth but a man is *challenged* by his offspring. As Lawrence Fishburne remarks in *Boyz 'n' The Hood,* any male can be a father but it takes a real man to be a dad. This is literally embodied in the relationship between the elements in their yin and yang forms.

Jing Kun or *Direct Officer* is as it sounds: a fair challenge. We may or may not have the resources to deal with it but it's straightforward, not underhand. The position of this character in the Ba Zi may indicate where to go for sound advice. Such a challenge ensures discipline and leads to influence. It is co-operative and trustworthy though it can overvalue status and over-represented, be complacent or fickle. These are the qualities of the public servant (in the family, a man's daughter).

Pin Kun on the other hand, *7 Killings,* is sometimes called the poison tongue, the word that can kill. In the Year pillar, expect a tricky relationship with parents; in the Day Branch (which represents true partner) late marriage. Only Water and Fire branches, because of their reversed polarity, offer a chance of jing kun here. Some Masters see pin kun as a corrupt official as well as a woman's lover (as opposed to husband). Pin kun has aspects of *por kwan,* the *broken soldier.* These are hard and subtle challenges. Mercy is short here though there is the flexible clarity essential in a leader of men. In the family this is a man's son. Kun balanced right, is pretty much equivalent to power.

**A Note About Power**: As Nietzsche wrote, "That which does not kill us, makes us stronger." Kun signifies discipline as well as challenge and power, and challenge and discipline so often lead to power. Kun is a kind of testing. Expect kun in the Ba Zi of any military or political leader. Jing kun is more empowering perhaps than pin kun because it's straightforward.

## *D. Jing Yan (Opposite Polarity) and Pin Yan (Same Polarity): Resource, Fuel, Support, Preparation, Education, Family, Parents*

Kun produces yan.

*Yan* represents family and tradition. Ideally this is found in the Year Pillar: Jing yan in the Year Branch means a diligent parent; diligent mother for a man (stem for a woman) but a preponderance of yan implies undue dependence. Sufficient yan suggests comfort, excess suggests laziness. A Ba Zi with 3–4 yan characters is likely to be strong, regardless of the timing of the Day Stem, but the strength will be of a different and less independent quality. Supporting elements should be chosen with this in mind.

Jing Yan (opposite polarity) is *Direct Resource* and represents the mother. This is unconditional love, safety, shelter from the storm. A Big Fate Pillar like this may be a period of respite after prolonged challenges. It is bonding, which Chuck Spezzano would say is identical to (and not the source of) effortless success. Jing Yan is good parenting. It is also, education, preparation, the tools of the trade and indeed appropriate training.

Jing yan in the year and month pillars can also speak of a family tradition. If it is Earth this may be religious or spiritual, Fire intellectual and/or Metal military, Water nautical/communicative.

Pin Yan (same polarity) is *Indirect Resource* and can identify a certain absence in or of parenting. If it's in the mother location (i.e. the year branch for a man, year stem for a woman) it may imply weak parenting. There is an odd inventiveness associated with pin yan and eccentricity but also a tendency to frustration – all of which may relate to *pin yan's* tendency to hands-off parenting. Pin yan can suggest an unsuitable or fractured education and poor judgement in what to rely upon. In the family it is father-in-law as well as stepmother. This might be fruitfully compared with the kun-choi relationship of father and son.

Pin yan can suggest poor judgement in whom to trust. A Ba Zi with too much may represent a gambler or a poor judge of character.

**Back to the Future**: eccentricity may not seem connected to hands-off parenting until we consider perhaps someone like the archetypical crackpot inventor Doc Brown in *Back to the Future*. Brilliant, eccentric and charismatic but would you entrust your kids to him? This is pin yan.

## *E.* Bay Gin *Friends (Same Polarity) and Gip Choi Rob Wealth (Opposite Polarity): Friends, Siblings, Peers, Rivals*

Yan produces bay gin.

*Bay gin* is the same element as the Day Stem. Bay gin itself is the same polarity while gip choi is the opposite.

Bay gin means *Friends*, often of the fair-weather variety. These relationships are essentially superficial. To have many of these characters suggests conviviality as opposed to profundity and (especially in the Day Branch) a lack of passion in relationship. A Day Stem with many bay gins is a networker but probably not a social climber. There is a lack of direction about it.

Bay gin in the Day Branch suggests a relatively sterile marriage or an inward-looking one with limited social life. This is doubly so if the stem and branch of the year are the same element also; this being the parental example. Often this means an arranged marriage. Bay gin in the year pillar suggests a closeness to parents as well as a family tradition; often religious or spiritual (if it is Earth), often intellectual (Fire), military (Metal), nautical (Water). Bay gin is the character of team-members rather than leaders and speaks of conviviality rather than excitement.

Gip choi (which means *Rob Wealth*) is a poorly chosen friend or wife. Such people are not what they seem. In the Year Pillar it suggests a powerful but not entirely positive parental example. If the Day Stem is yin this means it is overshadowed. If it is yang, it is competitive with the parent in question. In the Day Branch it suggests poor choice of partners; if in the Month and Year Branch as well, this is doubly so.

Gip choi is much more dynamic than bay gin but this is not a hardworking character; articulate but not necessarily trustworthy. Three or more of these in a Ba Zi speak of someone very convincing but who perhaps ought not to be believed. These people are go-getters but what they get may not rightly belong to them. They may gain the confidence in order to take. Since choi is wealth, gip choi is its loss hence also loss of wife. Gip choi in the hour branch may mean a spouse is traded in for a younger model (in the month branch, the reverse). Gip choi in Hour or Month can mean a friend steals your spouse. Knowing the difference between gip choi and bay gin can be crucial in mixing with our peers.

Bay gin is generally taken to represent the self as well as same gender siblings where gip choi is those of the opposite gender.

## 2. The Imperial Palaces

Another way to assess the qualities of the pillars is by way of the Palaces of the Stems, which broadly show us whether chi is alive or dead, frisky or sluggish. Over the centuries, meanings have become attached to the Palaces, offering us further information. That is the nature of 2000 years of calculation and experience.

### *A. Drafting the Palaces*

If you consult the grid *Finding the Palaces* in your drafting pack you will see a familiar pattern. Follow your finger for instance across the top row to geng 庚 the Yang Metal Day Stem. You may remember that 庚 probably represents a pair of hands pounding or possibly harvesting rice, by the way. Now follow your finger down to yuw 酉, (also you will remember, Metal) 酉 which lives at the Western Cardinal Point, the peak of Metal. Representing autumn and late afternoon, it is pure metal, consisting only of the two metal hidden stems geng 庚 and tsun 辛.

Now run your finger all the way across to the right where it reads "Dai Wong". Dai Wong means something like *commanding position* or *peak*. So, the Branch yuw 酉 the Rooster, sits at the Palace Dai Wong or the commanding position, for a Ba Zi with a geng 庚 Yang Metal Day Stem. Yuw 酉 is the peak of Metal. You knew this already.

The Palace Chang Sang means *birth*. Remember that the Branch jee/si the Snake 巳 holds a hidden Yang Metal stem 庚 to which it is said to be giving birth. Now run your finger up from yuw to the top Branch Character in the column. It is jee/si 巳 the Snake exactly as you'd expect. Again, follow your finger down to the row with "Mao" to the right, where the Branch in the geng 庚 column is chou 丑 the Ox. Mao of course means *tomb* and chou is the Tomb of metal. So, for a geng 庚 Yang Metal Day Stem, jee/si 巳 the Snake, occupies the Palace

Chang Sang or Birth, yu 酉 the Rooster occupies the Palace Dai Wong or peak and chou 丑 The Ox occupies the Palace of Mao the tomb.

These names describe the relative vitality of each Branch. The other Palaces are simply the states between birth and peak, peak and tomb and tomb and birth. This pattern applies to each of the Yang Day Stems. The pattern for a Yin Day Stem follows slightly different principles which we will rush past for the time being. We write these in the Palace Boxes down the column under the appropriate Branch. Now we know the quality of chi of each Branch.

### *B. The Significances of the Palaces*

What can we do with this information? The answer is that we now have something to add to what we know of the nature of the Ba Zi. Whatever characters we find above the Dai Wong are in some sense peaking. If they are over Chang Sang, they are in a sense experiencing birth (or rebirth), over Mao drawing on hidden resources and so on.

*Chang sang*: Birth, rebirth, vitality, intelligence, children, education, longevity, youthfulness. Can often signify a rapid change of character, situation or occupation. Chang sang under the Day Stem can often imply an ability to end something and restart, a self-re-invention, a re-boot. May imply travel; that is change of home. This last meaning will be confirmed by the Yik Ma Star and by an *empty* Water Palace. In the Life House it signifies beauty.

*Mo yuk*: Filthy Water. This character literally depicts dirty linen washed in public, suggesting scandal and as a rule, sexual politics. Multiple mo yuk pillars speak of serious issues with sexual ethics: infidelity and divorce. The Pillar it falls under will indicate when.

Under a Day Branch that changes element in combination, a very strong indicator, especially if the Day Branch does not support the Day Stem. Some Masters equate alcohol with dissolution and apply both to this Palace. In the Life House it indicates feckless character. In Month and/or Year Pillar applies to the circumstances of birth or youth. In Month Pillar could relate to the work environment.

*Koon tai*: Ascending. Childhood, growing and learning, playing, good health. Often a time of carefree fun which in the natural order of things would be childhood but can fall at any time of life. This speaks of physical, mental and moral health. A time of positive progress and regeneration. Indicates honesty; under the Day Pillar this may be self or spouse, under Year Branch parents, under Hour Branch children.

*Lum Kun*: Education. On the up, rising towards the peak. Often indicates formal learning, sometimes not so formal. Watch for indicators of a more abstract lesson (doubled Pillars for instance).

Accompanies *Sap Gon Luk* Special Star (see Module IV). When it coincides with *Man Cheung* Special Star it indicates further education (but only if there is enough Water) and adult education if under Day Stem. Under Year or Month Pillar, bright when young, also educated family. Under undesirable element: stubborn, resistant to instruction.

*Dai wong*: The Peak. Exciting and unstable, it doesn't hold. Can put a weak Day Pillar under strain. Success but of a fragile or short-lived kind. This relates to Hexagram 34 Da Zhuang: the question is not whether heights will be climbed but how the descent will be handled.

Often a life-defining experience, so note where it appears chronologically. Big success if under a supporting or required element. Too early (i.e. year or month); speaks of disappointment, a premature peak; possibly relating to parents.

*Shua*: Past the Peak. Start of decline, calm and steady. Often indicates some sort of loss. Under Month Pillar can indicate a lost physical skill. Under Year Pillar suggests early disappointment which can indicate a sickly or lost parent. Best under an unnecessary element which reduces the likelihood of important loss. With *Toe Far* Star can mean heartbreak. In Life House is a serious indicator of long-term frustration.

*Bang*: Sickness. Best of course under an unnecessary element. This is a weakening. May be literal illness (most likely if in Year Pillar) but may be a falling into decay. Applies also to parents in Year Pillar, self in Day Pillar. In Month Pillar may indicate a period of physical or other deterioration in 20s. The element (e.g. Metal = breathing) offers further information.

*Sai*: Death. Endings of all sorts including (but not limited to) the physical. The related element will offer clues. With sap san *yan* may apply to parents and so on. It could be the welcome exclusion of a contrary element. Can be literal death; identifying that is a special skill. It may apply either to the Branch or the Stem and polarity is important.

*Mao*: The Vault. This is where the Four Tombs fall, which indicates a storehouse or repository. Generally reckoned to hold money or choi. Each Tomb holds wealth for the Day Stems of a particular element. Choi of Day Stem ding 丁 for instance, is Metal and so it is Chou, Ox 丑 the Tomb of Metal that holds wealth. The Tomb wants to be clashed to release its bounty (by encountering another Tomb) but only once. Two clashes mean money in *and* out. It is worth taking time to locate Tombs and identifying how they may be clashed. Best also under a desirable element, especially if it is choi.

*Chua*: Despair. This is a very unhappy Palace if it appears under a necessary element. Under an undesired element it can be perfect, indicating the problem is over. A Fate Pillar over this may be a very quiet period of a person's life, not a time for risk taking.

*Toi*: Pregnant. A time of great potential when opportunities appear on the horizon. It is not, however, yet a time of success but one of vision and preparation. The element underneath will indicate the nature of the potential. Water suggests communication for instance and Wood movement or promotion. Too many of these indicates someone in constant need of help especially under Day Pillar or Life House. Together with an excess of yan it may be seriously needy although one appearance may simply be a cry for assistance.

*Yung*: Quickening. Further potential as Yung follows Toi and potential takes form, prior to its appearance at Chang Sang. Delicate but not alone. Under Day Stem suggests someone well-cared for.

**Important Note:** The impact of a Palace is weakened by a clash and strengthened by a combination in which the branch does not change element. If the element is needed, a positive impact is more pronounced; if not, a negative one is exacerbated.

### C. Further Significances: Empty Palaces

The table *Finding the Empty Palaces* represents this calculation. Obviously, it should be applied after the Palaces have been plotted. Find the Year Pillar, then follow your finger down to the foot of the page, where you will see in a separate box, the two Branches that sit in Empty Palaces. Repeat for Day Pillar and Life House and record in the box provided. Then apply the word *Empty* or Hung Mo (or if you're ambitious the Chinese characters) at the foot of each column wherein the relevant Branch appears.

**Important**: *This shows you which Branches are empty wherever they appear, and **not** necessarily in this pillar.*

### D. The Meanings of the Empty Palaces

The meaning of a Dead and Empty or *Hung Mo* Palace is tied in both with the element it qualifies and the related sap san. Having applied these there may be details of the individual Ba Zi that suggest a personalised implication. A negative indicator applying to an element that is best avoided for instance may be good news.

### E. Sap San Indications of Empty Palaces

So *Hung Mo bay gin/gip choi* indicates a time when our own personal power is diminished. Generally, this is undesirable but for overstrong Ba Zis, it may be just what is required (siblings – not much use).

*Hung Mo sik sun/zeun kun* indicates an estrangement from our children (and/or possibly work, creativity and purpose) as well as a weakening of the element that drains the self.

*Hung Mo choi* suggests a reduction in wealth but possibly also a relationship (for a man) that is off the rails. It can also mean a feeling of worthlessness.

*Hung Mo kun* suggests a reduction in influence but also perhaps of demands. This again is not necessarily negative. For a woman, however, it may indicate relationship difficulties.

*Hung Mo yan* is a distancing from parents as well as from resources; inadequate preparation, pointless learning, waste.

### *F. Purely Elemental Indications of Empty Palaces*

*Hung Mo* **Water** signifies travel, together with the Yik Ma star and/or the Chang Sang Palace it is close to irresistible. There are elemental cures for staying put, of course.

*Hung Mo* **Wood** implies broken bones. Together with the Yeung Yan Star it suggests injury. Best if Wood is unimportant.

*Hung Mo* **Fire** suggests a business taking off. A spectacular success is indicated, even better if Fire is choi or sik sun.

*Hung Mo* **Earth** suggests halting, slowing down possibly through illness.

Hung Mo **Metal** is the sound of metal percussion. It suggests fame especially in the performing arts.

> **Final Note concerning Empty Palaces:** some Masters see the characters identified as *Empty* being of no use. So, a Ba Zi showing Empty Rat and Ox cannot expect help from Rat or Ox colleagues or friends. For these purposes (which I don't necessarily endorse) it is more orthodox to draw them from Day and Year Branch only, e.g., not from the Life House. Some Masters (Joey Yap for instance) would say that even a positive Hung Mo bestows a certain emptiness to the experience.

# Module III: Clashes and Combinations

A Master once told me that nothing happens without a *clash*. Some feng shui professionals, however, think of a clash as inherently negative; some of the most baleful prognoses derived from Ba Zis focus on them. This is not strictly accurate. A clash (also sometimes referred to as *crash* or *crush*) is dynamic but whether it is negative (whatever that means in the great scheme of things) depends on many factors, principal among which is the strength of the day stem.

Exactly the same principles apply to whether a *combination* (see below) is supportive. *A combination is when two or more characters coincide and at least one changes element*. Furthermore, if we are to use the Ba Zi responsibly we are perhaps better advised to see any disturbance in elemental balance as a lesson waiting to be learned rather than a plague of frogs. A clash or combination between the characters of a Ba Zi can nonetheless totally change its nature. It is therefore essential to know how these work.

We will in the course of this module identify, Harms, Break-Ups, Alliances and Affinities – a list which will probably grow as you study beyond this course. But at the risk of repetition, let us be clear, at this stage, that when we refer to the Combinations of the Chinese Zodiac, we are referring to a relatively small number (actually four) of defined interactions whose outcome is a change of element for one or more of the combining characters.

Second, any comment about stem or branch can be applied to a year, a month, a day, an hour, (even a second) and/or a person or event ruled by the character. In time we will see that much the same is true in relation to locations and even buildings. Accordingly a Clash or Combination may occur when a Luck/

Fate or other Pillar becomes current, a new year, month or day dawns or even in conjunction with the site or facing direction of a new home. In a sense Ba Zi is simply feng shui without place. *Sam He* (or *Yang Gong)* feng shui is broadly Ba Zi on the ground.

Finally, although the term clash is generally interchangeable with crash or crush, the word *controlling* generally refers to the character that "wins" or "attacks". In other words, Wood might crush, clash or crash with Metal and vice versa but Metal *controls* Wood and not the other way round.

Having said all of that, there is actually no mystery about the way in which the Heavenly Stems and Earthly Branches interact, or at least no new mystery. The relationship between these characters is defined by elemental, astronomical and indeed agricultural rules just as is everything in Chinese Metaphysics. There is pretty much nothing in authentic feng shui that cannot be explained either in terms of Elemental interaction or the Trigrams of the *Book of Changes*.

The various Clashes and Combinations of the Branches are listed below and should be learned but in a sense that is to miss the point.

The key to mastery is in the *Hidden Stems.* You will recall that there is a sense in which the Branches are simply precise *cocktails* of stems these are the cocktails*:

---

* Not all Masters see the same configuration of Hidden Stems; Joey Yap for instance teaches that there are 28 – one for each of the 28 Lunar Mansions.

## The Twelve Earthly Branches with Hidden Stems

| Rat | Ox | Tiger | Rabbit | Dragon | Snake |
|---|---|---|---|---|---|
| 子 | 丑 | 寅 | 卯 | 辰 | 巳 |
| chee | chou | yan | muw | shun | jee |
| tze | chou | yin | muw | zhen | si |
| **Horse** | **Sheep** | **Monkey** | **Rooster** | **Dog** | **Pig** |
| 午 | 未 | 申 | 酉 | 戌 | 亥 |
| ng | may | shen | yuw | sute | hoi |
| wu | wei | shen | yuw | su | hai |

### Hidden Stems

| | | | | | |
|---|---|---|---|---|---|
| ren10 | quai9 | mow7 | jia10 | yi9 | wu5 |
| | tsun3 | bing7 | | quai3 | geng9 |
| quai20 | ji18 | jia16 | yi20 | wu18 | bing16 |
| bing10 | ding9 | ji/wu10 | geng10 | tsun9 | wu7 |
| ji 9 | yi3 | ren3 | | ding 3 | jia5 |
| ding11 | ji18 | geng17 | tsun20 | mow18 | ren18 |

There is an unmistakable pattern here: notice how the final Stem is carried forward. As generally with Chinese Metaphysics, there are exceptions (look closely at Tiger, Horse and Monkey). What is fascinating is to consider the relation between the rule and the exception. Note that the Earth Branches or *Tombs* all consist of Hidden Stems in the same ratio. Notice the resemblance between the Hidden Stem patterns of the Animals at the Cardinal Points. These are called "Toe Far" or *Plum Flowers*.

As you can see, the Rabbit is a cocktail of 1/3 Yyang Wood to 2/3 Yin Wood. The Stems, hidden and visible, combine and clash in keeping with rules which we shall encounter a little later. When these cocktails are understood, the Clashes and Combinations and their implications become obvious and learning by rote can actually get in the way of this.

Generally, Combinations are reckoned to take priority over Clashes; that is to say that if a Branch is involved in a Combination, it cannot simultaneously be clashed. Like all these rules, there are exceptions and indeed some Masters invoke an order of precedence which contradicts this convention. For flexibility of interpretation, simultaneously bearing all of these strictures in mind may be wisest.

Some Masters insist that all three Branches must be present for a *Triple Combination* to take place, others are less insistent. Some only see Combination in adjacent characters and some don't allow Combination with the Life House. For most the season is the clinching factor in these judgements. Some in point of fact don't draft a Life House. Our purpose is to learn Ba Zi rather than dogma, so I suggest we bear all of these approaches in mind as we interpret.

We will start with Branch combinations which are often considered more profound in meaning than those of the Stems.

Meanwhile let's have a brief look at *levels* of meaning.

## What Does It Mean for One Element to Combine to Another?

**Metal** combines to become **Water**: the words associated include *drain, draw out, milk, exhaust, melt, liquidate, express, own up, admit, flow.*

**Water** combines to become **Earth**: the words associated include *block, thicken, stick, impede, settle, silence, civilise, obey, contain.*

**Water** combines to become **Wood**: the words associated include *manifest, take shape, seed, emerge, bear fruit, take up a position, solidify, poetry, step up.*

**Water** combines to become **Fire**: the words associated include *prosper, win, breakthrough, let go, soar, flare, fly, passionate relationship, independence, self-sufficient.*

**Wood** combines to become **Fire**: the words associated include *inspire, express, shine, emerge into the light, ignite, promote, is frank, burn.*

**Wood** combines to become **Earth**: the words associated include *success, marriage, procreate, settle down, self-sufficient, abundant.*

**Wood** combines to become **Metal**: the words associated include *self-harm, compete, perfectionist, changing sides, suborned, pressure to excel, OCD.*

**Fire** combines to become **Water**: the words associated include *extinguish, drown, slake, compromise, taming, discourage, explained, coming clean.*

**Fire** combines to become **Wood**: the words associated include *restricted, retrogressive, reclusive, timid, return home, reversal, supported, empowered, Mother, safety.*

**Earth** combines to become **Water**: the words associated include *loosen, free, dissolve, liberating.*

**Earth** combines to become **Fire**: the words associated include *inspired, self-sufficient, released, indiscreet, unself-critical, liberal, open, retrospective, pressure, return to roots.*

**Earth** combines to become **Wood**: the words associated include *exploited, self-destructive, restless, manic, rapid, flexible, ambitious.*

**Earth** combines to become **Metal**: the words associated include *prosperous, creative, fertile, fickle, circular.*

**A Note About Language**. One of the keys to interpretation is identifying the *level* of significance. Just as choi can mean wife or money so when Metal clashes Wood we might expect the Metal to for example assault the Wood or fashion it. In one Ba Zi one of these might be relevant, in another one, the other. The trick is to find words that in some senses mean the same but would never appear on the same page of a thesaurus.

## What Does It Mean for One Element to Clash or Control Another?

**Metal** clashes **Wood**: words associated include *cut, fashion, shape, add value, improve, whittle, carve, exploit, assault, makes explicit.*

**Water** clashes **Fire**: words associated include *dampen, snuff out, suppress, profit, exploit, flood, takeover, democracy, consultation, rule of law.*

**Wood** clashes **Earth**: words associated include *harvest, exploit, dig, take advantage, plant, feed.*

**Fire** clashes **Metal**: words associated include *melt, liquidate, tame, puzzle, reasoning, witnessing, pause.*

**Earth** clashes **Water**: words associated include *pollute, solidify, reclaim, put plans into action, swamp, drought.*

Notice that all pure clashes express a kun/choi relationship, that is discipline bringing advantage, risk leading to profit, daring leading to love and so on. This is far from inherently negative. As I said, nothing happens without a clash.

## Branch Clashes and Combinations

*When two or more characters coincide and at least one changes element.*

There are three principal groups of Branch combinations. These are:

**The Triple Combinations**
**The Seasonal Combinations or *Frames***
**The Two Combinations, also known as the *Secret Friends* or the *Six Harmonies.***

### *1. The Triple Combinations (Branch characters 120° apart)*

**The *Triple* Combinations**

| | | |
|---|---|---|
| shen | chee | shun |
| (shen | tze | zhen) |
| 申 | 子 | 辰 |
| **Monkey** | **Rat** | **Dragon** |
| hoi | muw | may |
| (hai | muw | wei) |
| 亥 | 卯 | 未 |
| **Pig** | **Rabbit** | **Sheep** |
| yan | ng | sute |
| (yin | wu | su) |
| 寅 | 午 | 戌 |
| **Tiger** | **Horse** | **Dog** |
| jee | yuw | chou |
| (si | yuw | chou) |
| 巳 | 酉 | 丑 |
| **Snake** | **Rooster** | **Ox** |

What do these combine to and why? For an answer, let us examine the Hidden Stems of the Branches…
Here is the Rat:

Chee
(Tze)
子

| | | | |
|---|---|---|---|
| **Rat** | | **Yang Water** | |
| 壬 | **10** | yum (ren) | Yang Water |
| 癸 | **20** | quai | Yin Water |

The Rat is 1/3 Yang Water to 2/3 Yin Water. The 30-day Rat month consists literally of ten days Yang Water followed by twenty Yin Water.

Generally, the final Hidden Stem is considered to reveal the identity of the Branch and is termed *pure*; this pure phase is reckoned the most powerful. The Rat is 100% Water, the only Branch of which this is true. Logically then, it sits at midwinter (or midnight) when Water is at its peak. There are more complete esoteric accounts, but nothing is wetter than the Rat.

In short, because it is all Water it stands to reason that it should be predisposed to influence other Branches to turn to Water and with one exception, indeed it does. Broadly these comments apply (in a variety of ways) to a person with a Rat branch in their Ba Zi, a Rat hour, day, month, year or Fate Pillar, even a building sitting due North.

What this *means* depends of course like pretty much everything else in the Ba Zi, on the Day Stem. Notice, however, that the involvement of the Rat in a Triple Combination to Water does not change the Rat.

Now let's look at the Monkey which of course along with the Dragon, also combines with the Rat to make Water.

Shen
(shen)
申

| **Monkey** | | **Yang Metal** | |
|---|---|---|---|
| 己戊 | **10** | ji | Yin Earth/Wu Yang Earth |
| 壬 | **3** | ren | Yang Water |
| 庚 | **17** | gung | Yang Metal. |

The Monkey is said to *give birth* to Water because it is at the beginning of the Metal season when Water is born. Again, this predisposes it to influence other Branches to turn to Water. Four of the Branches (Tiger, Snake, Monkey and Pig, the so-called *Stations*) are, you will recall, said to give birth to the next element in the productive sequence i.e., of the next season.

Notice that the Monkey's middle Hidden Stem is Yang Water. These apparently short-lived middle stems are the key to the Triple Combinations. Notice also that the dominant Hidden Stem is Yang Metal which suggests that in other circumstances, Shen will be involved in combination to Metal.

Monkey, unlike the Rat, is changed by this Combination. Metal of course gives birth to and is *expressed* by Water. This is *sik sun* or creativity. So, Monkey changing to Water may become more creative, more expressive, perhaps harder working. A female Monkey may (depending on other factors) literally give birth.

What About the Dragon?
shun
(zhen)
辰

| **Dragon** | | **Yang Earth** | |
|---|---|---|---|
| 乙 | **9** | yi | Yin Wood |
| 癸 | **3** | quai | Yin Water |
| 戊 | **18** | wu | Yang Earth |

The Dragon is one of the four Earth Branches, otherwise known as the *Four Vaults* or *Four Tombs* which share a complex and often powerfully creative mutual relationship. The Tombs are the key to identifying times of wealth in the Ba Zi. The question that concerns us here, however, is what the Dragon vault contains.

The answer again is in the apparently insignificant middle Hidden Stem: quai Yin Water. Because it is yin, quai completes the combination with the Yang Water within Shen and the pure Water of Chee. The initial Yin Wood of course implies some disposition to Wood.

Although how the Day Stem responds is more important, combining to Water is for the Dragon, a Combination to choi, that is the element controlled, crushed, crashed or clashed by the Dragon. For both genders this means success, money and possessions. For a male Dragon it also means mistress. The choi is technically pin choi or same polarity. The opposite polarity jing choi of course means wife.

## The *Triple* Combinations with Hidden Stems

| | | | | | | |
|---|---|---|---|---|---|---|
| Shen | | Chee | | Shun | | |
| (shen | | tze | | zhen) | | |
| 申 | | 子 | | 辰 | | |
| **Monkey** | | **Rat** | | **Dragon** | | **combine to Water** |
| 戊己 | 10 | 壬 | 10 | 乙 | 9 | 水 |
| 壬 | 3 | | | 癸 | 3 | |
| 庚 | 17 | 癸 | 20 | 戊 | 18 | |

| | | | | | | |
|---|---|---|---|---|---|---|
| hoi | | muw | | may | | |
| (hai | | muw | | wei) | | |
| 亥 | | 卯 | | 未 | | |
| **Pig** | | **Rabbit** | | **Sheep** | | **combine to Wood** |
| 戊 | 7 | 甲 | 10 | 丁 | 9 | 木 |
| 甲 | 5 | | | 乙 | 3 | |
| 壬 | 18 | 乙 | 20 | 己 | 18 | |

| | | | | | | |
|---|---|---|---|---|---|---|
| yan | | ng | | Sute | | |
| (yin | | wu | | su) | | |
| 寅 | | 午 | | 戌 | | |
| **Tiger** | | **Horse** | | **Dog** | | **combine to Fire** |
| 戊 | 7 | 丙 | 10 | 辛 | 9 | 火 |
| 丙 | 7 | 己 | 9 | 丁 | 3 | |
| 甲 | 16 | 丁 | 11 | 戊 | 18 | |

| | | | | | | |
|---|---|---|---|---|---|---|
| jee | | yuw | | chou | | |
| (si | | yuw | | chou) | | |
| 巳 | | 酉 | | 丑 | | |
| **Snake** | | **Rooster** | | **Ox** | | **combine to Metal** |
| 戊 | 5 | 庚 | 10 | 壬 | 9 | 金 |
| 庚 | 9 | | | 辛 | 3 | |
| 丙 | 16 | 辛 | 20 | 己 | 18 | |

Some consider that these Triple Combinations only take place when all three characters are present. Others detect combination as long as the Cardinal character (the toe far) is involved and others are less rigid again. A skilled diviner will conclude on the basis of the case in hand.

All four Triple Combinations work in the same way. These are generally considered the strongest and most inevitable combinations. We will discuss the precedence of the clashes and combinations later.

## *2. The Directional or Seasonal Combinations or Frames*

| | | | |
|---|---|---|---|
| hoi<br>(hai)<br>亥<br>**Pig** | Chee<br>(tze)<br>子<br>**Rat** | Chou<br>(chou)<br>丑<br>**Ox** | **Northern**<br>**Water**<br>水 |
| yan<br>(yin)<br>寅<br>**Tiger** | muw<br>(muw)<br>卯<br>**Rabbit** | shun<br>(zhen)<br>辰<br>**Dragon** | **Eastern**<br>**Wood**<br>木 |
| jee<br>(si)<br>巳<br>**Snake** | ng<br>(wu)<br>午<br>**Horse** | may<br>(wei)<br>未<br>**Sheep** | **Southern**<br>**Fire**<br>火 |
| shen<br>(shen)<br>申<br>**Monkey** | yuw<br>(yuw)<br>酉<br>**Rooster** | sute<br>(su)<br>戌<br>**Dog** | **Western**<br>**Metal**<br>金 |

The characters grouped around the Cardinal Points (or *Plum Flowers*) combine to make the element of that Season. Again, many consider that they only combine when all three are present. For many, the Season of the Month Branch (winter, spring, summer, autumn) is the clincher. The Animal characters are connected by the adjacent Hidden Stems. The pure or *remainder* chi at the end of each is, as we have noticed, repeated at the beginning of the next. Seasonal Combinations are reckoned weaker than Triple.

| | | | | | | |
|---|---|---|---|---|---|---|
| jee | | ng | | may | | Southern |
| (si) | | (wu) | | (wei) | | Fire |
| 巳 | | 午 | | 未 | | 火 |
| **Snake** | | **Horse** | | **Sheep** | | |
| 戊 | 5 | 丙 | 10 | 丁 | 9 | |
| 辛 | 9 | 己 | 9 | 乙 | 3 | |
| 丙 | 16 | 丁 | 11 | 己 | 18 | |

## 3. *The Two Combinations*

### (Sometimes Called, *Secret Friends* or *Six Harmonies*)

### The Two Combinations or *Six Harmonies*

| | | |
|---|---|---|
| chee | | chou |
| (tze) | | |
| 子 | | 丑 |
| **Rat** | **with** | **Ox** |
| hoi | | yan |
| (hai) | | (yin) |
| 亥 | | 寅 |
| **Pig** | **with** | **Tiger** |
| sute | | muw |
| (su) | | |
| 戌 | | 卯 |
| **Dog** | **with** | **Rabbit** |
| yuw | | shun |
| | | (zhen) |
| 酉 | | 辰 |
| **Rooster** | **with** | **Dragon** |
| shen | | jee |
| | | (si) |
| 申 | | 巳 |
| **Monkey** | **with** | **Snake** |
| may | | ng |
| (wei) | | (wu) |
| 未 | | 午 |
| **Sheep** | **with** | **Horse** |

For some schools of thought, the Secret Friend is the *amulet* of the year. The one-forward, one-back pattern on the clock face is easy to remember and may record an agricultural rationale. The term *Harmony* may relate to the ancient correlation between feng shui and the pentatonic scale. These, the last true Branch combinations, are a little perverse. There is a bending out-of-shape to them. We might even call them reluctant.

**A Note About Secret Friends**. The earliest practitioners of feng shui, the *di li* or *kan yu* men, working before the "south-facing stone" (that is magnet and therefore compass) had been identified) would place a *shih stick* in the ground to ascertain orientation. The shih stick cast a shadow and when it was shortest the sun was at its height. From this they could ascertain directions. What they observed was that the light pattern for the hour immediately before the zenith mirrored the pattern of the hour immediately afterwards and the next one mirrored the hour before that. This would pair Horse with Sheep and Monkey with Snake. Something similar is true of the monthly light patterns either side of the Summer Solstice. It may well be that the Secret Friends embody this connection.

| | | | |
|---|---|---|---|
| chee<br>(tze)<br>子 | | chou<br><br>丑 | |
| **Rat** | **with** | **Ox** | **makes earth** |

The Rat is turned to Earth by the Ox. But why to Earth? The Yin Earth of the Ox of course is not fertile without Water but a flooded meadow is no use to anybody. Consider the season.

| | | | | | |
|---|---|---|---|---|---|
| chee | | chou | | | |
| (tze) | | | | | |
| 子 | | | 丑 | | |
| **Rat** | | **with** | **Ox** | | **makes earth 土** |
| 壬 | **10** | | 癸 | **9** | |
| | | | 辛 | **3** | |
| 癸 | **20** | | 己 | **18** | |

The Rat and the Ox are joined by a common Yin Water stem. In a Rat year, the Ox has privileges. Under the Ox, the Rat often follows another's agenda, typically that of an Ox. Otherwise, the Ox (of small blockages) may get in the way. Something similar is true of Dragon and Rooster:

| | | | | | |
|---|---|---|---|---|---|
| yuw | | shun | | | |
| | | (zhen) | | | |
| 酉 | | 辰 | | | |
| **Rooster** | | **with** | **Dragon** | | **makes metal 金** |
| 庚 | **10** | | 乙 | **9** | |
| | | | 癸 | **3** | |
| 辛 | **20** | | 戊 | **18** | |

The Rooster is typically glamorous and superficial, while the Dragon is more intense. This combination speaks of distraction. The Arthurian story of Merlin and Nimue is Dragon/Rooster. The old wizard is led away from his path by his lust for the young nymph. In a Rooster year the Dragon is distracted from his purpose; often by glittering Yin Metal of which money may be an example, compare Samson and Delilah.

## The Two Combinations or *Six Harmonies*

| | | | |
|---|---|---|---|
| chee<br>(tze)<br>子 | | chou<br>丑 | |
| **Rat** | **with** | **Ox** | **makes Earth 土** |
| hoi<br>(hai)<br>亥 | | yan<br>(yin)<br>寅 | |
| **Pig** | **with** | **Tiger** | **makes Wood 木** |
| sute<br>(su)<br>戌 | | muw<br>卯 | |
| **Dog** | **with** | **Rabbit** | **makes Fire 火** |
| yuw<br>酉 | | shun<br>(zhen)<br>辰 | |
| **Rooster** | **with** | **Dragon** | **makes Metal 金** |
| shen<br>申 | | jee<br>(si)<br>巳 | |
| **Monkey** | **with** | **Snake** | **makes Water 水** |
| may<br>(wei)<br>未 | | ng<br>(wu)<br>午 | |
| **Sheep** | **with** | **Horse** | **makes Fire 火** |

The Six Harmonies actually perpetuate an astronomical conjunction: when the sun and moon converge in Zhen the handle of the Big Dipper points to Yuw. When the sun and moon converge in Yuw the Dipper's handle points to Zhen. And so on. The seven visible and two invisible stars of the Big Dipper or Ladle (part of Ursa Major) dictate also the movement of the Flying Stars of San Yuen Feng Shui as well as the procession of the tai sui. In addition, each pairing is associated with a planet of the solar system. We've examined this connection before of course.

## <u>The Two Combinations with Planetary Association</u>

| | | | | |
|---|---|---|---|---|
| hoi | | yan | | |
| (hai) | | (yin) | | |
| 亥 | | 寅 | | |
| **Pig** | **with** | **Tiger** | **makes Wood 木** | **Jupiter** |
| sute | | muw | | |
| (su) | | | | |
| 戌 | | 卯 | | |
| **Dog** | **with** | **Rabbit** | **makes Fire 火** | **Mars** |
| Chee | | chou | | |
| (tze) | | | | |
| 子 | | 丑 | | |
| **Rat** | **with** | **Ox** | **makes Earth 土** | **Saturn** |
| yuw | | shun | | |
| | | (zhen) | | |
| 酉 | | 辰 | | |
| **Rooster** | **with** | **Dragon** | **makes Metal 金** | **Venus** |
| shen | | jee | | |
| | | (si) | | |
| 申 | | 巳 | | |
| **Monkey** | **with** | **Snake** | **makes Water 水** | **Mercury** |
| may | | ng | | |
| (wei) | | (wu) | | |
| 未 | | 午 | | |
| **Sheep** | **with** | **Horse** | **makes Fire 火** | **Moon/ Sun** |

Derek Walters sees this as a demonstration that the *wu xing* precedes the Four Elements of Empedocles. Be that as it may, the Two Combinations are among the indivisible essentials of the Ba Zi and at the heart of a number of procedures combining Ba Zi and feng shui. Of which more later…

## Branch Clashes

There are three principal groups of Branch clashes. These are:

**Diametrical Opposition**
**The Six Harms**
**The Six Destructions, also known as the *Break-Ups*.**

## The Branch Clashes (180° i.e. Diametrical Opposition)

Again, clearly derived from Elemental rules. Note that yin clashes only with yin and yang only with yang. These are the only true branch clashes.

| | | | |
|---|---|---|---|
| chee | | ng | |
| (tze) | | (wu) | |
| 子 | | 午 | |
| **Rat** | **clashes** | **Horse** | **Yang 水 Water clashes Yang 火 Fire** |
| chou | | may | **In the hidden stems** |
| | | (wei) | 辛 clashes 乙 |
| 丑 | 未 | | |
| **Ox** | **clashes** | **Sheep** | **Yin 土 Earth clashes Yin 土 Earth** |
| yan | | shen | |
| (yin) | | | |
| 寅 | | 申 | |
| **Tiger** | **clashes** | **Monkey** | **Yang 火 Wood clashes Yang 金 Metal** |
| muw | | yuw | |
| 卯 | | 酉 | |
| **Rabbit** | **clashes** | **Rooster** | **Yin 火 Wood clashes Yin 金 Metal** |
| shun | | sute | **In the hidden stems** |
| (zhen) | | (su) | 癸 clashes 丁. |
| 辰 | | 戌 | |
| **Dragon** | **clashes** | **Dog** | **Yang 土 Earth clashes Yang 土 Earth** |
| jee | | hoi | |
| (si) | | (hai) | |
| 巳 | | 亥 | |
| **Snake** | **clashes** | **Pig** | **Yin 火 Fire clashes Yin 水 Water** |

So, what is it to clash? The Sap San character kun which represents the element that wins or is proactive in a clash (if you will *controls*) means *influence* and *discipline* as well as something like *attack.* Clash can be annihilation for a weak Ba Zi, i.e. one that is not timely (that is within its natural season) or poorly supported. But it can mean a win despite adversity for a strong one. It can be a challenge that makes a strong Ba Zi or the last straw of a weak one. The key to understanding this is the Day Stem.

Each clash has a particular nature:

| | | | |
|---|---|---|---|
| Chee | | ng | **A put down, disappointment,** |
| (tze) | | (wu) | **dampening, realism, stimulus,** |
| 子 | | 午 | **ideas, provocation.** |
| **Rat** | **clashes** | **Horse** | **Yang 水 Water clashes Yang 火 Fire** |
| chou | | may | **Tetchiness, rivalry (often** |
| | | (wei) | **among women), stubbornness,** |
| 丑 | | 未 | **strategic withdrawal, dispute over beliefs.** |
| **Ox** | **clashes** | **Sheep** | **Yin 土 Earth clashes Yin 土 Earth** |
| yan | | shen | **Youthful aggression, pedantry,** |
| (yin) | | | **male violence, road rage,** |
| 寅 | | 申 | **necessary protest, revolution.** |
| **Tiger** | **clashes** | **Monkey** | **Yang 火 Wood clashes Yang 金 Metal** |
| muw | | yuw | **Argument, bitchiness, mistrust,** |
| | | | **sexual, jealousy, winning** |
| 卯 | | 酉 | **at all costs, letdown,** |
| | | | **professional competition, fraud.** |
| **Rabbit** | **clashes** | **Rooster** | **Yin 火 Wood clashes Yin 金 Metal** |
| shun | | sute | **Physical confrontation, major** |
| (zhen) | | (su) | **obstruction, reason vs intuition** |
| 辰 | | 戌 | **bloody-minded, stands on principle.** |
| **Dragon** | **clashes** | **Dog** | **Yang 土 Earth clashes Yang 土 Earth** |
| jee | | hoi | **Reduction of mobility, injury** |
| (si) | | (hai) | **to the legs, road, sea and air** |
| 巳 | | 亥 | **traffic accidents and delays,** |
| | | | **caution, discretion, conscience.** |
| **Snake** | **with** | **Pig** | **Yin 火 Fire clashes Yin 水 Water.** |

# Harms and Destructions

## *A: The So-called Six Harms*

### The Six Harms

| | | |
|---|---|---|
| chee<br>(tze)<br>子<br>Rat | may<br>(wu)<br>未<br>Sheep | Invisible antagonists:<br>Horse 午 and Ox 丑 |
| yan<br>(yin)<br>寅<br>Tiger | jee<br>(si)<br>巳<br>Snake | Invisible antagonists:<br>Pig 亥 and Monkey 申 |
| shen<br>申<br>Monkey | hoi<br>(hai)<br>亥<br>Pig | Invisible antagonists:<br>Tiger 寅 and Snake 巳 |
| chou<br>丑<br>Ox | ng<br>(wu)<br>午<br>Horse | Invisible antagonists:<br>Rat 子 and Sheep 未 |
| Muw<br>卯<br>Rabbit | Shun<br>(zhen)<br>辰<br>Dragon | Invisible antagonists:<br>Dog 戌 and Rooster 酉 |
| sute<br>(su)<br>戌<br>Dog | yuw<br>酉<br>Rooster | Invisible antagonists:<br>Rabbit 卯 and Dragon 辰 |

The Six Harms are a sort of counterpoint to the *Six Harmonies*. Each *Harm* is inevitable because of firmer alliances already entered into. The Rat opposes the Sheep because the Sheep is diametrically opposed to the Ox, the Rat's *secret friend*. Equally the Rat opposes the Horse. Add to that that they are members of elementally opposed directional combinations; they were never going to get on, were they? The way the harm plays out is that it involves or pertains to a third party or a loyalty that is being conflicted, often literally centred on the *invisible antagonists*. Like so much conflict, it's not about what it appears to be about. Proxy wars are typical.

## *B: The Six Destructions (or Break-Ups)*

| | | |
|---|---|---|
| **chee** | **yuw** | |
| **(tze)** | | **Water drains Metal** |
| 子 | 酉 | |
| **Rat** | **Rooster** | |
| **shen** | **jee** | |
| | **(si)** | **Water drains Metal** |
| 申 | 巳 | **also, Secret Friends** |
| **Monkey** | **Snake** | |
| **shun** | **chou** | |
| **(zhen)** | | |
| 辰 | 丑 | **Water drains Metal** |
| **Dragon** | **Ox** | |
| **ng** | **Muw** | |
| **(wu)** | | **Fire drains Wood** |
| 午 | 卯 | |
| **Horse** | **Rabbit** | |
| **yan** | **hoi** | |
| **(yin)** | **(hai)** | |
| 寅 | 亥 | **Fire drains Wood** |
| **Tiger** | **Pig** | **also Secret Friends** |
| **sute** | **may** | |
| **(su)** | **(wei)** | |
| 戌 | 未 | **Fire drains Wood** |
| **Dog** | **Sheep** | |

The Six Destructions relate to "Triggers" and the propensity for Branches to combine cyclically. The relationship these pairs have in common is technically a *drain* rather than a clash and the drain may be more pernicious after being reinforced by a triple combination. So, Destructions are more about a threat, a potential problem than an actual confrontation and therefore not generally ranked high priority in the hierarchy of clashes and quasi-clashes. They include two pairings that are actually also Harmonies. Some call these clashes *The Six Break-Ups* which can be quite literal.

## The Clashes and Combinations of the Stems

The impact of the Heavenly Stems is sometimes thought of as less profound than that of the Branches. Some consider that the Stems deal with the superficial, the apparent and the venal as opposed to the spiritual. The combination rules that apply to them are relatively simple:

### The Heavenly Stems

| | | | | |
|---|---|---|---|---|
| Gap | yute | bing | ding | mow |
| (jia) | (yi) | | | (wu) |
| 甲 | 乙 | 丙 | 丁 | 戊 |
| **yang** | **yin** | **yang** | **yin** | **yang** |
| **wood** | **wood** | **fire** | **fire** | **earth** |
| gay | gung | tsun | yum | quai |
| (ji) | | | (ren) | |
| 己 | 庚 | 辛 | 壬 | 癸 |
| **yin** | **yang** | **yin** | **yang** | **yin** |
| **earth** | **metal** | **metal** | **water** | **water** |

**Stem Combinations**

| | | |
|---|---|---|
| Jia combines with ji | | **to make Earth 土** |
| **甲** | **己** | |
| **yang** | **yin** | |
| **wood** | **earth** | |
| Yute (yi) | combines with gung | **to make Metal 金** |
| **乙** | **庚** | |
| **yin** | **yang** | |
| **wood** | **metal** | |
| bing | combines with tsun | **to make Water 水** |
| **丙** | **辛** | |
| **yang** | **yin** | |
| **fire** | **metal** | |
| ding | combines with ren | **to make Wood 木** |
| **丁** | **壬** | |
| **yin** | **yang** | |
| **fire** | **water** | |
| mow (wu) | combines with quai | **to make Fire 火** |
| **戊** | **癸** | |
| **Yang** | **yin** | |
| **earth** | **water** | |

**Notice the order**: the Cycle of Production and that (as with the Branches) yin only combines with yang and vice versa. Consider the impact of a Day Stem involved in such a combination. Add sap sans to that and you suddenly know an awful lot about a Ba Zi. See pp. 17–18 in the Chinese Calendar.

## Stem Clashes

**Stem clash rules are even simpler:** they follow the Cycle of Destruction and only like polarities clash. The simplicity of these rules as we will see, underlies the conventions of Branch clashes.

**The Elemental Values and Polarity of the Ten Heavenly Stems**

| | 甲 | 乙 | 丙 | 丁 | 戊 |
|---|---|---|---|---|---|
| **Cantonese** | Gap | yute | bing | ding | mow |
| **Pin Yin** | **jia** | **yi** | bing | ding | **wu** |
| **Element** | wood | wood | fire | fire | earth |
| **Polarity** | **yang** | yin | **yang** | yin | **yang** |

| | 己 | 庚 | 辛 | 壬 | 癸 |
|---|---|---|---|---|---|
| **Cantonese** | gay | gung | tsun | yum | quai |
| **Pin Yin** | **ji** | geng | sun | **ren** | **gui** |
| **Element** | earth | metal | metal | water | water |
| **Polarity** | yin | **yang** | yin | **yang** | yin |

**Stem Clashes**

1. Only with same polarity.
2. Follows normal clashing rules, i.e. Metal clashes Wood, Wood clashes Earth, Fire clashes Metal, Earth clashes Water.

*Gung* clashes *gap*, *gap* clashes *mow*, *mow* clashes *yum*, *yum* clashes *bing*, and *bing* clashes *gung*... and so on...

And that's it.

## Further Clashes, Affinity Groups, etc.

### *A: Self-Clashes*

The Following Branches do not play nicely among themselves:

| | | | |
|---|---|---|---|
| shun | hoi | ng | yuw |
| (zhen) | (hai) | (wu) | |
| 辰 | 亥 | 午 | 酉 |
| **Dragon** | **Pig** | **Horse** | **Rooster** |

The way the clash develops reflects the nature of the animal. So, a Dragon with a Dragon partner or in a Dragon year may have ego issues. A Pig may feel crowded by another Pig nearby (the Chinese character for *home* is one Pig under a roof: not two) or in a Pig year. A Horse may sense their spontaneity restricted when having to share the spotlight in a Horse year. A Rooster may experience loyalty and fidelity issues in a Rooster year (like 2017 or over shorter time scales).

### *B: Ingratitude Clash I*

In a Rat Year the Rabbit risks the *Ingratitude Clash.* At such a time a Rabbit may question the value of their heritage and the Rat may find their generosity falling on stony ground. There is a sense of overwhelm and lack of proportion in this Clash.

**Ingratitude Clash I**

| | | |
|---|---|---|
| Muw | clashes | chee(tze) |
| 卯 | | 子 |
| **Rabbit** | | **Rat** |

## *C: Ingratitude Clash II*

Some term the conjunction of Monkey, Tiger and Snake an *Ungrateful Punishment* which is a related idea. In a Monkey year, say, a person with a Ba Zi containing Snake and Tiger Pillars (especially if one is the Day Pillar) may feel unappreciated. The dynamic is that historical help has not been acknowledged. Being cast adrift and homelessness are traditional indicators. At least two of the Pillars should be adjacent.

**Ingratitude Clash II (*Fire Penalty*)**

| | | | | |
|---|---|---|---|---|
| Yan (yin) | clashes | shen | clashes | jee (si) |
| 寅 | | 申 | | 巳 |
| **Tiger** | | **Monkey** | | **Snake** |

Some instead call this pattern a *Fire Penalty* and expect interference by a third party: gazumping, unsolicited advice, triangular relationships, rigged elections; pretty much endemic in 2022 (especially February and May) and again in 2025. Since all these Animals are "Stations", problems with transport and mobility are inherent.

## Other Conventional Patterns: Affiliations, Alliances, Crosses

Generally, these categories do not involve characters changing element and so are not true combinations. They are more to do with the way that characters do or do not co-operate. They are less hardwired into Ba Zi Rules as representing discoveries made by Masters over the millennia.

### *A: Directional Houses or Affiliations*

**Directional Houses or Affiliations**

| | | |
|---|---|---|
| **chee (tze)** | **chou** | **<u>The House of Ingenuity</u>** |
| **子** | **丑** | **Joined by Yin Water:** |
| **Rat** | **Ox** | **communication, routine.** |
| Plots | Executes | |
| **Yan (yin)** | **muw** | **<u>The House of Progress</u>** |
| **寅** | **卯** | **Joined by Yang Wood:** |
| **Tiger** | **Rabbit** | **aspiration, growth.** |
| Hunts | Charms | |
| **Shun (zhen)** | **jee (si)** | **<u>The House of Enchantment</u>** |
| **辰** | **巳** | **Joined by Yang Earth:** |
| **Dragon** | **Snake** | **withdrawal, secrecy.** |
| Conjures | Packages | |
| **ng (wu)** | **may (wei)** | **<u>The House of Seduction</u>** |
| **午** | **未** | **Joined by Yin Fire:** |
| **Horse** | **Sheep** | **sticking and splitting.** |
| Attracts | Entertains | |

| | | |
|---|---|---|
| **shen** | **yuw** | <u>**The House of Business**</u> |
| **申** | **酉** | **Joined by Yang Metal:** |
| **Monkey** | **Rooster** | **profit and precision.** |
| Calculates | Sells | |
| **sute** | **hoi** | <u>**The House of Homemaking**</u> |
| **(su)** | **(hai)** | |
| **戌** | **亥** | **Joined by Yang Earth:** |
| **Dog** | **Pig** | **loyalty and consistency.** |
| Guards | Arranges | |

These cooperate easily because they are neighbours joined by Hidden Stems. These patterns are central to compatibility analysis and team building as well as assessing fortunes in a particular time period. How will the Rat fare in the Ox year? (Answer: he will continue to plot but he may rely on the Ox for the outcome.) Above all though they are helpful in seeing how an individual varies uniquely from any stereotype we may be tempted to impose.

Note, however, that as we shall learn in Module IV, there may be further conjunctions to consider. Dog and Pig are for instance a mutual *Gip Sat*.

Not all adjacent pairings work: the Dragon is said to lose money at the appearance of the Rabbit for instance. Sense can always be made of these simply by referring to the elemental relationships.

## *B: The Three Crosses**

These very powerful four-way alliances consist of Branches not otherwise comfortable together. The limitation of an incomplete cross is defined by the character(s) missing. Remember, by the way, that the most acute of us may sometimes offer an interpretation that is *completely* wrong because we opt for the yang rather than yin significance or vice versa: to the untidy person it is not that tidiness is not an issue but that it has been neglected rather than embraced.

### i. The Four Plum Flowers

| **The Four Plum Flowers** | |
|---|---|
| **Chee (tze)**<br>**子**<br>**Rat** | **Communication, strategy.** |
| **muw**<br>**卯**<br>**Rabbit** | **Aspiration, ease with the powerful, an ability to contain fear, to charm, networks.** |
| **Ng (wu)**<br>**午**<br>**Horse** | **Extroversion, sheer sexuality, spontaneity, improvisation.** |
| **yuw**<br>**酉**<br>**Rooster** | **Show, fashionableness, the look of things, accounting.** |

* *I was taught this by Derek Walters whose term this is.*

The grouping consists of two incompatible pairs: the Four Cardinal Compass Points, each the relative Plum Flower or *irresistible* star for a group of the remaining animals: those in the Triple Combination whose element is produced by the toe far.

The Rooster for instance is toe far for the Animals of the Water Triple Combination, Monkey, Rat and Dragon. A Ba Zi with such a grouping of such unstoppable charm is very unusual. For all four to show in a chart speaks of great passion and great charisma.

### ii. The Four Earths: Literary or Creative Cross (aka the Four Vaults or Tombs)

| | | | |
|---|---|---|---|
| **Chou**<br><br>**丑**<br>**Ox**<br>Completes | <br><br>**Persistent**<br>**autocratic.** | **Shun**<br>**(zhen)**<br>**辰**<br>**Dragon**<br>Magical creativity | <br><br>**Egotistical,**<br>**risk taker.** |
| **may**<br>**(wei)**<br>**未**<br>**Sheep**<br>Team player | <br><br>**Attends to the**<br>**needs of others.** | **sute**<br>**(su)**<br>**戌**<br>**Dog**<br>Guards | <br><br>**Loyal, once**<br>**committed.** |

The individual relationships here are very uneasy. Each Branch is the *Vault* of a particular Day Stem so the relationship with the Day Stem is particularly important. The Earth Branches are the key to wealth in a Ba Zi.

### iii. The Four Stations, Terminals or Stables

| | |
|---|---|
| **Yan**<br>**(yin)**<br>**寅**<br>**Tiger**<br><br>Predatory | **Dissolves obstacles, fearless.** |
| **jee**<br>**(si)**<br>**巳**<br>**Snake**<br>Curious | **Creates opportunity.** |
| **shen**<br>**申**<br>**Monkey**<br><br>Hands on | **Drives, services engines,**<br>**solves practical problems.** |
| **hoi**<br>**(hai)**<br>**亥**<br>**Pig**<br>Home-loving | **Demands security but**<br>**often has itchy feet.** |

These are the Branches that give birth and what they have in common is a propensity for novelty and especially movement. Their presence in a Ba Zi speaks of mobility issues, positive or negative. As we know already for instance, the coincidence of Pig and Snake suggests stasis. Logically, the solution to the Fire Penalty is the Pig.

## Hybrid Combination/Clashes

### *A: Bullying Punishment*

| | | |
|---|---|---|
| may | sute | chou |
| (wei) | (su) | |
| 未 | 戌 | 丑 |
| **Sheep** | **Dog** | **Ox** |

This shows just how precarious the *Four Earths* alliance is. For a Ba Zi that is already Earth-heavy or for some other reason not in need of Earth, this can be very damaging indeed. Earth is just immoveable. The *Bullying Punishment* is simply the Four Earths without the Dragon. It's missing the unique transformational power of the Dragon.

The Bullying Punishment is stuck-ness without solution. There are other metaphors (such as houses that won't sell); Raymond Lo relates this to various forms of morbidity. It can also be a pattern of chronic abuse. Very common for obvious reasons in 2018, 2021 and again in 2027.

If Dog, Ox and Sheep are the Year, Month and Day Branch (in no particular order) of someone's Ba Zi you are may be dealing with someone who had a very hard time at school.

## *B: Push Me-Pull You, Multipurpose Combination and Destruction*

**Push me-pull you**

| | | |
|---|---|---|
| **Shen** | **jee** | **combine to Water and clash** |
| | **(si)** | |
| 申 | 巳 | |
| **Monkey** | **Snake** | |
| **yan** | **hoi** | **combine to Wood and clash** |
| **(yin)** | **(hai)** | |
| 寅 | 亥 | |
| **Tiger** | **Pig** | |

These are destructive relationships, star-crossed lovers and that sort of stuff. Romeo was probably a Monkey (attracted to metal, prone to ingenious solutions) and Juliet a Snake (calls on magic from a third-party, not sure whether she's serious or not, the Sorcerer's apprentice). Jon Snow is a Snake. Don Quixote is a Horse, Sancho Panza a Sheep, etc. Try this with your favourite soap opera to remind yourself that we are dealing with a species of archetype here.

# Module IV: Special Stars or *Sans Sats*

The san sats (literally *favourable/unfavourable*), sometimes called *Compound* or *Symbolic Stars* or *Fairies and Devils* are derived from observation of certain combinations and clashes over a period of centuries of Ba Zi drafting. They are in effect another form of summary like sap sans, lap yums and the Life House and each focuses certain characteristics of the Ba Zi.

Some are quite predictable and simply summarise an elemental relation (man cheung) or duplicate a Palace (sap gon luk). Some are in effect simply sap sans. Others bring important new information and all bring an additional perspective. Some at least (like toe far) can be calculated in space as well as time for use in feng shui.

As ever, the power and influence of each is reduced or altered by clashing, draining or combining as well as by the Palaces and their emptiness (or not) and the related sap san. It's all a question of nuance, so I have made no attempt to examine their significance exhaustively. I am sure as you practise you will discover new meanings.

There are several hundred san sats of which I routinely calculate about twenty. The following may be the most readily applicable.

## Heavenly Gifts

The first five stars are derived from the *Heavenly* Stem (as opposed to the *Earthly* Branch) which implies that they are the gifts of Heaven; gifts of grace, perhaps. Remember though that the Chinese have never thought of Heaven as presided over by an old man with a white beard or the domain of angels and cherubs. What is meant by Heavenly providence is best thought of as being as opposed to Earthly or Human providence.

**Note:** all but one san sat in this group is **derived from the Day Stem**, although some can be derived additionally from the Year Stem.

### *1. Tin Yute Gwai Yan – the Nobleman Star*

Tin yute gwai yan (literally *Eastern Guardian*) sometimes called *the Star of Aid* is usually derived from the day stem (**see table below**) when its meaning is very personal. It can, however, just as easily be derived from the year stem which is likely to be more general, more immediate and more literal. Derived this way (or from the day stem of the first day of the year depending on the system) it is much used in year prediction when it implies a certain benevolence.

The tin yutes come in pairs attached to different characters in the Ba Zi. Often interpreted as the presence of a mentor or helping hand, usually male, generally older, and reckoned not to be a member of the family, tin yute frequently denotes an important teacher coming into a person's life. Tin yute – with the usual nuances – also implies consistently sound health.

As with every aspect of the Ba Zi, if we look at these meanings more deeply, the quality of information deepens. How does the tin yute combine or clash? Which characters are involved? Is it actually helpful?

Every Ba Zi has two tin yute stars but where they are located often indicates an attitude to assistance. Sometimes they cover two or more whole Pillars, sometimes only a pair of years, widely separated. This suggests on the one hand a smoother life with plenty of helping hands, on the other a certain independence. When tin yute appears in the current year or Fate Pillar it accompanies promotion and increased wealth (especially in a choi year, if choi is supportive).

Coinciding with other stars can colour it also: with yik ma (see below), tin yute indicates a profitable move and so on. In a jing choi year (for a man) or jing kun year (for a woman) marrying a partner who represents tin yute for you means they will be supportive.

The polarity and element of the character it is attached to of course, offer further information. If the element is useful, so is the Nobleman and vice versa. Some people, however, just don't want to be helped: a Sheep with tin yute attached to an unwanted element is stuck indeed. For others tin yute can be the cavalry arriving when all seems lost.

| | | | | | | | | | | |
|---|---|---|---|---|---|---|---|---|---|---|
| **Stem:** | 甲 | 乙 | 丙 | 丁 | 戊 | 己 | 庚 | 辛 | 壬 | 癸 |
| **Tin Yute:** | 未丑 | 申子 | 酉亥 | 酉亥 | 未丑 | 申子 | 未丑 | 寅午 | 卯巳 | 卯巳 |

## *2. Man Cheung – the Scholarly Star*

Man cheung relates to further or higher education. It is a measure of intellectual or academic quality which relates to the place it appears in the Ba Zi: if it is in the Day Pillar there is superior intelligence,* in the Year Pillar a tradition of education, in the Hour Pillar, smart kids and so on. In the Big Fate it could signal a certain change of character, a chastening perhaps. Generally, we expect the Ba Zis of academics, writers and researchers to feature this star.

Traditionally, where it appears in the Four Pillars, further education can be assumed, *but generally only if it is under a supportive element and there are sufficient water characters present* #. If man cheung is in the Year Pillar which of course covers the years from birth to 16 (and there is enough Water present), further education is likely to take place early; if in the Month Pillar a little later.

In the Day Pillar, adult or lifelong education is suggested. If there is no Water, education may turn out to have been disturbed or incomplete. Combinations to and from Water of course add further meaning. Man cheung can suggest introversion, excess man cheung a certain arrogance. Palace and sap san colour and nuance these meanings.

Again, this star can be derived from Year or Day Stem and each yields a different level of meaning. It is the Star of *expression* or *sik sun*.

| | | | | | | | | | | |
|---|---|---|---|---|---|---|---|---|---|---|
| **Stem:** | 甲 | 乙 | 丙 | 丁 | 戊 | 己 | 庚 | 辛 | 壬 | 癸 |
| **Man Cheung:** | 巳 | 午 | 申 | 酉 | 申 | 酉 | 亥 | 子 | 寅 | 卯 |

\# At least three is the traditional requirement.
* Could be the spouse!

### 3. *Yeung Yan – the Power Star*

The second half of the yeung yan ideograph is actually a knife. For a fertile woman some interpret this as the delivery of a child. Otherwise, it is often seen as an intrusive medical operation, accident or even wound. Some indeed call yeung yan the *Terrorist* or *Angry Star*. Presumably, a terrorist is at least to a great extent powered by anger. And it does often appear to coincide with anger-management issues; some would make connections between these levels of meaning.

If for instance we map onto this character Ron Smothermon's *Integrity States#* which are instructions for becoming fully conscious, we might call yeung yan the state of the soul or mind that he terms *Emergency*, which is characterised by impatience. A person in this state will just want to get on with things and may therefore cut corners to do so and risk all sorts of chaos. Perhaps a terrorist is inherently like this. An examination of Osama Bin Laden's issues with his parents would be an interesting document.

Some map sexual politics onto the character. If the Ba Zi of a childless woman shows a prominent yeung yan, she may be quite bitter. An implication of this, which I simply relate without endorsing one way or the other, is that an infertile woman is inherently dissatisfied and that the yeung yan star telegraphs this distress.

A weak Ba Zi is said to be strengthened by yeung yan, a strong one weakened. When yeung yan is controlled by kun, its aggressive energy is focused, leading to a competitive even a military leadership gift. Excess pin kun turns this double-edged sword ruthless or even self-destructive.

Together with sap gon luk, yeung yan implies a clinically focused mind. Together with choi it can mean disability (often in my experience involving Yin Metal). Choi changing to gip choi on meeting yeung yan is reversal of fortune. When over sai, chua and bang palaces, yeung yan warns of pierced flesh: in the

Hour Pillar of poor relations with offspring, in the Day Pillar an intolerant and possibly sickly spouse, Month Pillar eccentricity, Year Branch poor judgement of risks. This is essentially the Gip Choi (aka *Goat Blade*) Star.

**Stem:** 甲 乙 丙 丁 戊 己 庚 辛 壬 癸

**Yeung Yan:** 卯辰 (寅) 午未 (巳) 午未 (巳) 酉戌 (申) 子丑 (亥)

**(The alternate character in brackets is often considered more powerful.)**

#*Winning through Enlightenment* and *Transforming Number 1.*

**A Note About Immeasurably Ancient Practices**: Yeung Yan, the Goat Blade – the literal meanings of the Chinese Ideographs – speaks of poor timing, hurry, a failure to respect the Tao. We can all feel the right moment and the right location. When we don't, we risk injury. The characters perhaps remind us of the deep history of these ideas: a blade implying literal cutting, perhaps originally a literal blood sacrifice.

## 4. *Sap Gon Luk – the Star of Fame*

Sap gon luk speaks of effortless success and especially fame but not necessarily wealth. Sap gon luk means literally *multiple prospects* and always coincides with the *lum kun* (Education) palace which makes of course for an implication here of success merited by hard work.

When it appears in the Day Pillar this star is often a sign of an especially successful person. In the Year it can mean that the parents or grandparents were notable and/or that there was early success with a premature peak. Sometimes sap gon luk positioned thus in the past can make for tension and frustration. Sap gon luk in the Hour Pillar of course suggests both success at work later in life and children with great potential.

In each of these cases, character, element and polarity will offer more clues as to the nature of the gift.

Sap gon luk strengthens a weak Ba Zi. If it is not clashed it signifies consistent help from family but clashed, sap gon luk speaks of helplessness and eviction. A clashing year or Fate Pillar may bring bankruptcy.

Elementally of course it is mostly bay gin, so sap gon luk overloads a strong Ba Zi. Accordingly, as bay gin clashes choi, in an overstrong Ba Zi, sap gon luk also implies a disadvantaged wife and father.

In an unbalanced Ba Zi: funny looking, mean-spirited.

With yum san: a gamble that may or may not pay off!

At Empty Palace, serious money loss. Essentially the corresponding Branch with sap san polarity reversal.

| | | | | | | | | | | |
|---|---|---|---|---|---|---|---|---|---|---|
| **Stem:** | 甲 | 乙 | 丙 | 丁 | 戊 | 己 | 庚 | 辛 | 壬 | 癸 |
| **Sap gon luk:** | 寅 | 卯 | 巳 | 午 | 巳 | 午 | 申 | 酉 | 亥 | 子 |

### 5. *Hong Yim Sat – the Home Wrecker*

This implies that you are short-changing your partner. You are dissatisfied and seek compensation elsewhere. This may not be (but usually is), overtly sexual and so is important to flag. Because it is always derived from the Day Stem, words can usually change this largely emotional and spiritual trap. There is a very good chance that all the action here is in the head, a sympathetic ear may be able to keep it that way.

Some Masters see this star as describing exclusively unmarried people, which may simply be a cultural anachronism.

It is inevitable that this person is in pain. If you are sensitive to these things, you will know this already. Fundamentally, no one is a victim of anything, I suggest, but this and the following star suggest that the two illusory states they flag, manifest separately. Both suggest a careless, irresponsible view of relationship. Blame is apportioned. Everything is someone's fault. This star accompanies affairs, messy divorces, marital strife and so on. It is worst when it coincides with mo yuk palace. Hexagram 44 may tell you more.

This is obviously enough, one of the stars you need to learn to present in a way that use can be made of it. There are times when it shows in the Day Pillar of a younger person for instance, when you can warn of this possibility so as to have it show up in a less damaging way.

Equally, its appearance in the Year Pillar implies a parental pattern that may inform future behaviour but could be salutary. Clashes and combinations within the Pillars may change its nature. It follows that it may be mitigated by timely intervention with the correct element.

To summarise, hong yim is about the subject's dissatisfaction in relationship. Interestingly, this appears to be the same calculation as Lily Chung's *Scholar Star.* Go figure!

| | | | | | | | | | | |
|---|---|---|---|---|---|---|---|---|---|---|
| **Day Stem:** | 甲 | 乙 | 丙 | 丁 | 戊 | 己 | 庚 | 辛 | 壬 | 癸 |
| **Hong yim sat:** | 午 | 午 | 寅 | 未 | 辰 | 辰 | 戌 | 酉 | 子 | 申 |

## *6. Loy Hong Yim Sat – the Roving Eye*

This implies that your partner is deceiving you. It is the precise physical counterpart of hong yim sat: the calculation and table below are identical except that Loy hong is derived from the Year Stem.

The tendency may now have become physical. If so, finger-pointing may be involved. It is usually the partner who is misbehaving in an unsubtle, physical way. Some Masters (used to) say this is simply hong yim within wedlock; again, society seems to have overtaken such cultural prejudices. What's for sure is that blame is among the most self-disempowering of emotional choices.

This is a potentially very distressing star that must be handled with compassion. There may be actual misbehaviour. Feng shui cures include the placing of an image of a hen (not a Rooster! Think about it…) above the toilet. Obviously, also it can be deliberately combined or clashed away with strategic timing and placing.

To summarise, loy hong is about the dissatisfaction of the subject's partner in relationship.

| | | | | | | | | | | |
|---|---|---|---|---|---|---|---|---|---|---|
| **Year Stem:** | 甲 | 乙 | 丙 | 丁 | 戊 | 己 | 庚 | 辛 | 壬 | 癸 |
| **Loy hong:** | 午 | 午 | 寅 | 未 | 辰 | 辰 | 戌 | 酉 | 子 | 申 |

## Earthly Powers

These are derived from the Earthly Branches, Day or Year, which may mean they are especially deeply rooted.

### *1. Jeung Sing – the Leading Star*

Jeung sing is a state of refusing to be second best. The qualities associated with it include competitiveness and impatience. The won't-be-second-best star often speaks of a marriage in which priorities are skewed but equally often implies Number Two going for the top job or a habitual employee setting out on his or her own. You can be sure that under jeung sing, the unsatisfactory situation will not persist.

In the Year Pillar it implies aspirational and possibly demanding parents (that will be clarified by the relationship with the Day Pillar of course). In a balanced Ba Zi, jeung sing in the Day Pillar signifies leadership abilities. If it is an unfavourable element, however, it implies abuse or misunderstanding of power.

Jeung sing arriving in the Year or the Fate Pillar brings opportunities for the entrepreneur. Aggression (which literally means *stepping forward*) is the attribute most often associated with jeung sing.

Generally derived from the Day Branch. Elementally, this is a Star of solidarity (not quite bay gin though). This is the corresponding Plum Flower – which may make it some sort of paradigm.

| | |
|---|---|
| **Branch:** | 子丑寅卯辰巳午未申酉戌亥 |
| **jeung sing:** | 子酉午卯子酉午卯子酉午卯 |

## 2. *Wah Koi – the Star of Arts*

Wah koi: clever but lonely. Wah koi is the *Magnificent Crown*, under Day or Year Branch suggests someone exceptionally gifted who is not sociable. The person is likely to be introverted and bookish and may excel at study especially music, literature and philosophy but probably not commerce. Not a team-player, the wah koi Day Pillar may sometimes appear stand-offish, even arrogant. They learn rapidly and can be very creative, retaining information and recycling it. They may, however, be reclusive and privately unhappy. These qualities, celibacy and withdrawal into a life of contemplation, are particularly common when the star is in the Hour or later Fate Pillars. If wah koi is in the Day Pillar, marriage may not suit them; in the Year Pillar the parents may have been somewhat hands-off. Generally derived from the Day Branch, wah koi is the Vault or Tomb of the Branch, possibly then someone living in a cloister.

**Branch:** 子丑寅卯辰巳午未申酉戌亥
**Wah koi:** 辰丑戌未辰丑戌未辰丑戌未

### 3. *Yik Ma – the Racehorse Star*

Yik ma sometimes called the *Voyager*, or Travelling Horse, is related to the Four Stations Team of Snake, Monkey, Tiger and Pig whose common quality is movement. Every yik ma Star is one of these four.

The ideograph is itself a horse. Wherever it appears, yik ma indicates moving house or occupation and a certain restlessness. It is the escape star. This can be defused by travelling instead of moving house; conversely the energy can be induced by careful positioning and timing; this is *sam he* feng shui. The Pillar it appears in suggests when the movement will take place. Multiple appearances identify someone as inveterately restless or nomadic. The Day Pillar may suggest a foreign-born spouse or one whose work takes them away from home and under the Fate Pillar a term of residence abroad.

When yik ma clashes, the sense of mobility may be unwished-for and uncomfortable. Associated element indicates rationale for movement.

Can be derived from Day (more personal) and/or Year Branch (more cosmetic). A more complex calculation exists.

| | |
|---|---|
| **Branch:** | 子丑寅卯辰巳午未申酉戌亥 |
| **Yik ma:** | 寅亥申巳寅亥申巳寅亥申巳 |

## 4. *Gip Sat – the Devil Star*

Gip Sat (which means *Robbery Curse*) is at the very least an agent of delay. If gip sat is at jing choi in the Day or Year Pillar and is supportive there may be a susceptibility to robbery. If kun (for a woman) is not supportive and gip sat at Day Pillar, unhappy marriage. Best for people who live by their wits, a very unsafe and unstable star, especially so with yeung yan. Best to see this restricted to individual years rather than spanning a whole Pillar. At the least it implies delays and interruptions. Can be derived from Day or Year Branch.

| | |
|---|---|
| **Branch:** | 子丑寅卯辰巳午未申酉戌亥 |
| **Gip Sat:** | 巳寅亥申巳寅亥申巳寅亥申 |

## 5. *Mong San – the Hidden Star*

For some Masters *mong san* is underhand, a cheat, a character denoting craftiness and prejudice. In this perspective mong san, under the Day Pillar of a strong Ba Zi suggests someone who commands respect, although intimidating and hard to construe. Under the Day Pillar of a weak or unbalanced Ba Zi it implies poor temper, grudges and addictive, lowlife types of activity. The persuasive and plausible mong san Day Pillar with tin yute may enjoy financial success in the law, literature or the arts.

A more traditional reading of mong san indicates danger from one or more elements during the Pillar concerned. If in the Year, childhood may be fraught with particular dangers. There are ten varieties of mong san. Each suggests a hidden weakness or vulnerabilityt:

**Yang Wood mong san** suggests danger from trees and upright objects. Such people are often best suited to cities, (but not high rise – agoraphobia, fear of aspiration).

**Yin Wood mong san** danger from grass and herbs. Such a person should never smoke.

**Yang Fire mong san** suggests danger from the sun and from heat. Often unsuited to direct sunlight. Not keen on limelight.

**Yin Fire mong san** suggests danger from fire. Often such people have a fascination with matches. A need for privacy.

**Yang Earth mong san** suggests danger from the earth. Often such people are (rightly) frightened of caves and/or heights. Major blockages including tumours are possible.

**Yin Earth mong san** suggests danger from smaller obstructions. Minor blockages including benign tumours are possible.

**Yang Metal mong san** suggests danger from cars and fires. Such people should drive with great care.

**Yin Metal mong san** suggests danger from scissors and knives. Such people should take care with saws, knives and cutlery and iPhones.

**Yang Water mong san** suggests danger from the sea. Such people should not take up surfing or yachting. Blurting is a weakness.

**Yin Water mong san** suggests danger from small bodies of water. Take care swimming and bathing and keeping confidences.

Mong San suggests appropriate vigilance. Keep a child with a Yin Metal mong san Year Pillar away from the knife drawer! Can be derived from Day or Year Branch.

| | |
|---|---|
| **Branch:** | 子丑寅卯辰巳午未申酉戌亥 |
| **Mong San:** | 亥申巳寅亥申巳寅亥申巳寅 |

### *6. Toe Far – the Irresistible*

Sometimes called the Plum Flower Star. The same calculation is used for the Plum Blossom position in a home where traditionally plum flowers are placed in order to attract a partner.

This Star relates to charisma and irresistibility of all sorts but for a Chinese Master sexual irresistibility is often the priority. Under the Day Stem (and I quote) *Partner always pleases you*. With pin choi, mistress rather than wife is connoted but beauty is indicated either way. In the Hour Pillar it indicates affairs within marriage.

Mo yuk is the toe far palace, that is to say the one following chang sang in the sequence of palaces. In a strong (that is to say secure) palace, toe far is gregarious and generous and especially suitable for schmooze-friendly vocations such as sales, politics and PR. In a weak Ba Zi or over a poor palace, these can be lazy, venal lay-abouts. On the other hand, the very strongest toe far suggests a world leader. Go figure.

**Internal toe far,** i.e. toe far under a supporting element, sex will be satisfying and within marriage.

**External toe far** (under an unsupportive element) is outside marriage.

**Salty Toe Far** (Wandering Palms) with hong yim, lack of boundaries.

**Toe Far gip sat**: nasty, Michael Hutchence/David Carradine (allegedly).

**Toe Far yik ma**: playing away.

**Yum san** with **Toe Far**: relationship built on sand, crumbles accordingly.

**Toe Far** with **man cheung** and **wah koi**: stars, artists, performers.

**Toe Far** with **yik ma** at **dai wong:** pimp! Earnings from women.

**Toe Far crashing:** stds especially with poor san sat like gip sat.

Can be derived from Day or Year Branch. Toe far is always found at the Cardinal Points, the Relationship Branches.

| | | | | | | | | | | | | |
|---|---|---|---|---|---|---|---|---|---|---|---|---|
| **Branch:** | 子 | 丑 | 寅 | 卯 | 辰 | 巳 | 午 | 未 | 申 | 酉 | 戌 | 亥 |
| **Toe Far:** | 酉 | 午 | 卯 | 子 | 酉 | 午 | 卯 | 子 | 酉 | 午 | 卯 | 子 |

## Sleeping Stars

These are derived from the Year Branches, which may mean their effect is superficial, blatant, physical and/or unconscious. In any case deep-seated relationship issues are indicated.

### *1. Goo San – the Lone Star*

Goo San under the Day Pillar indicates someone, usually a man, wilfully single who may or may not be aware of their choice. Often divorced or widowed, they are "once bitten twice shy". Two goo sans suggest a monk, nun or celibate, particularly with wah koi.

Male goo san with female qua suk should sleep separately. Some Masters say this conjunction can otherwise be life-threatening.

Psychologically this suggests a relationship past its sell-by date where either partner may choose any alternative including morbidity as a preference. Relationship workshops are often populated by people with goo san, wah koi and qua suk in their later Fate Pillars. If these san sats appear in the Day or current Big Fate Pillar, you do the subject a favour by questioning deeply any claim they make to seeking or wishing to maintain intimate relationship.

Derived from Year Branch. These are the *Station* Branches. As this is a pure *sam he* calculation, some Masters add the Vault from the same Triad as a second goo san.

| | |
|---|---|
| **Branch:** | 子丑寅卯辰巳午未申酉戌亥 |
| **Goo San:** | 寅寅巳巳巳申申申亥亥亥寅 |

## 2. *Qua Suk – the Lone Starlet*

Qua suk is very much the yin goo san. Under the Day Pillar it usually indicates a woman who sleeps alone. Often divorced or widowed, they can be quite content with their own company and may eventually re-marry. On the other hand, under the Day Pillar of a single woman of a certain age, qua suk can signal dissatisfaction.

Male goo san with female qua suk (and vice versa) should sleep separately. Some Masters say that qua suk is life-threatening and should be *cured* by deliberate combination. Some female diviners disagree with this possibly Confucian conclusion.

Derived from Year Branch. These are again the Tombs or Vaults – which may be an important distinction.

| | |
|---|---|
| **Branch:** | 子丑寅卯辰巳午未申酉戌亥 |
| **Qua Suk:** | 戌戌丑丑丑辰辰辰未未未戌 |

### *3. Yum San – the Broken Star*

Yum San is about separation and bonding: the *Draining Star*.

One diviner defined it to me as *lady who looks like a man* and vice versa. Yum san is inherently unbalanced; a multiplicity of this star often coincides with unbalanced physiology: overgrown features, truncated lower half of body, pipe-cleaner legs etc. Under Year or Day Pillar, may coincide with disability especially if Yin Metal is present.

Yum san is rebellious and contrary. There are constant issues with rights and entitlements especially with parents and authority. Yum san is the drunk in the dole queue. In the extreme, may attack or injure their parents or vice versa. Sai and chua Palaces exacerbate.

Uncorrected, yum san is a loser. Psychologically, this might be termed the *unbonded star*.

**A Note About Yum San:** I give you the name under which I was first introduced to this star. Truth is that the pin yin terms are *Yuen Zhen*. Both are very evocative: yuen means original, authentic, traditional and it is probable that the Mongol Emperor Kublai Khan intended those overtones when giving his dynasty that name. Its astrological meanings however include "neck" with the implication of execution. Perhaps his Chinese advisers intended those too. Zhen is the character for the astrological Dragon. So we can venture a meaning something like "executioner of the Dragon". There are those who would insist that I'm quite wrong but as a diviner, I find it quite persuasive.

Derived from the Year Branch via a calculation that comprehends the effect of a yin birth in a yang year and so on. This may make gender issues inherent.

| | | |
|---|---|---|
| **Branch:** | **子丑寅卯辰巳午未申酉戌亥** | |
| **Yum San:** | **未申酉戌亥子丑寅卯辰巳午** | **yang born in yang year, yin in yin year** |
| | **巳午未申酉戌亥子丑寅卯辰** | **yang born in yin year, yin in yang year** |

## Lucky Stars: the Mighty Duks

These three Lucky Stars triangulate a person's lucky purple patches. When all three coincide it's time to back an outsider on the Derby!

| | | | |
|---|---|---|---|
| **1.** | **Tin duk** | **Blessings of Heaven** | **Heaven chi** |
| **2.** | **Yute duk** | **Blessings of the Moon** | **Earth chi** |
| **3.** | **Yute yeung** | **Monthly Leader** | **Human chi** |

Tin duk, the *Star of Benevolence* and yute duk the *Star of Kindness*, are both powerful and very much a pair, even more fortuitous when found together. Tin duk is yang, yute duk yin.

With tin duk the sun smiles on you, life is stable and the outlook sunny. With yute duk, the magical mysterious, feminine moon is your illumination and you are said to survive disasters unscathed.

Yute yeung *Monthly Leader*, speaks of good choices. All three derive from the Month Branch, which may link to Western Astrology, as may Life House, Big Fate and Solar Fortnights.

Finding any of these under Day or Year Pillar is seriously fortuitous and a Fate Pillar over these is well-augured for its duration. Every Ba Zi has them; more fortunate ones cover longer stretches of time, less fortunate a single year; which is the moment to compete against the odds or take risks that might not otherwise be worth taking.

Remember also that like every san sat, these stars appear under the relevant character within the Cycle of Hours, Days and Months as well as Years. When personalising fortuitous days, the duks should be a major consideration. It is worth manoeuvring to gain their benefit.

Yute yeung spans a division of the Western Zodiac, even more powerful than the duks. When Yute yeung is resource, and *yan* helpful, a fortune will be made; at zeun kun when it is supportive, you can get away with anything. It's worth calculating times when all three coincide; it doesn't happen in all Ba Zis.

| | | | | | | | | | | | | |
|---|---|---|---|---|---|---|---|---|---|---|---|---|
| **Month Branch:** | 子 | 丑 | 寅 | 卯 | 辰 | 巳 | 午 | 未 | 申 | 酉 | 戌 | 亥 |
| **Tin Duk:** | 巳 | 庚 | 丁 | 申 | 壬 | 辛 | 亥 | 甲 | 癸 | 寅 | 丙 | 乙 |
| **Yute Duk:** | 壬 | 庚 | 丙 | 甲 | 壬 | 庚 | 丙 | 甲 | 壬 | 庚 | 丙 | 甲 |

| | | | | | | | |
|---|---|---|---|---|---|---|---|
| **Solar Fortnight:** | **(after)** | *yu soi* | *chun fun* | *kuk yu* | *siu mun* | *ha gee* | *dai shu* |
| **Yute Yeung:** | | 亥 | 戌 | 酉 | 申 | 未 | 午 |
| **Solar Fortnight:** | **(after)** | *chu shu* | *chow fun* | *zeun gong* | *siu shuut* | *dung gee* | *dai hohn* |
| **Yute Yeung:** | | 巳 | 辰 | 卯 | 寅 | 丑 | 子 |

## Fiu Gong – the Chancer Star

Fiu gong is a risk taker. This star at the Day Pillar means the subject will be *a billionaire or go to jail* as a temple diviner told me. The appearance of the fiu gong in a Pillar is no guarantee that the risk will bear fruit but this person is said to be so indomitable that they are unafraid of ghosts, their willpower is unshakeable and their personality extraordinarily tough.

Fiu gong attaches only to certain Dogs and Dragons, the two yang vaults, the first of which holds Fire, the second Water. A yang vault is likely to be larger and accordingly bear a greater reward than a yin one, of course. Any vault needs clashing but only once or its contents are lost. Some call this second clash *in-tomb* chi.

Most agree that there are only four possible fiu gong Pillars, but authorities differ as to which they are.

| | | | | |
|---|---|---|---|---|
| **Fiu Gong:** | 庚 | 庚 | 戊 | 戊 |
| **Pillars (1)** | 辰 | 戌 | 辰 | 戌 |

| | | | | |
|---|---|---|---|---|
| **Fiu Gong:** | 庚 | 庚 | 壬 | 戊 |
| **Pillars (2)** | 辰 | 戌 | 辰 | 戌 |

## And Finally ... Yang Edge

Taoist thought tends to concern process rather than end: the Hour of the Horse is not 12 noon but the double hour from 11 a.m. to 1 p.m. It was not until the T'ang that luo p'ans depicted three Mountains at each of the eight compass points.

If we draw the Hexagram gou *Poison* (Number 18) which depicts scorpions fighting in a jar and implies painful emotional, psychological and spiritual *stuff*, the Western mind tends to recoil. Seen through the prism of the Tao, however, this is a fortuitous image which speaks of taking arms against a sea of troubles, to coin a phrase. By the same token, Hexagram 34 Da Zhuang *Great Strength*, might seem benevolent but the fact is that all of the changing lines are about what we do with power while it lasts. The yang edge is a species of san sat or symbolic star which embodies this principle.

Yang edge applies to a yang day stem born at the peak of its element:

**Yang Edge**

| Day Stem | Month | Clash | Solution |
|---|---|---|---|
| gap | muw | yuw | zhen |
| 甲 | 卯 | 酉 | 辰 |
| yum | chee | ng | yan |
| 壬 | 子 | 午 | 寅 |
| gung | yuw | muw | sute |
| 庚 | 酉 | 卯 | 戌 |
| bing | ng | chee | chou |
| 丙 | 午 | 子 | 丑 |
| mow | ng | chee | chou |
| 戊 | 午 | 子 | 丑 |

The yang edge represents a fragile, over-the-top kind of strength. It actually illustrates why in Ba Zi, strong is not necessarily desirable nor weak undesirable. Both are unbalanced and yang edge is precarious.

This is a dependent, brittle kind of strength vulnerable to underhand competition. Being of the same element as the Day stem it represents bay gin/gip choi or superficial relationship, fair-weather friends.

The moment to watch for is when the yang edge is clashed (because it is over-strong, it is over-reactive and will provoke massive retaliation). The cure is to neutralise the clashing element with one it combines with – which is a ploy worth attempting in many Ba Zis and not just in relation to yang edge. The box above shows my usual solutions.

# Glossary

| | |
|---|---|
| Ba zi: | Literally "Eight Images", that is Four Pillars |
| Bang: | "Sickness", the name of the seventh of the Twelve Palaces |
| Bay gin: | Sap San "Friend", describes a character in a Ba Zi that is of the same element and polarity as the Day Stem |
| Bing: | The third of the Heavenly Stems, signifying Yang Fire |
| Chang sang: | Birth, the first in the sequence of Palaces |
| Chee: | Cantonese for the Mandarin "tze", meaning the astrological Rat, the first Branch in the sequence of hours |
| Chia: | Mandarin for the second Heavenly Stem signifying Yang Wood (= gap) |
| Choi: | Sap San "Wealth", as in "gung hei fat choi". |
| Chou: | The Ox |
| Chow: | Autumn |
| Chua: | Tenth Palace signifying "Despair" |
| Chu: | Limit (as in, "of Heat") |
| Chun: | Spring |
| Dai: | Great |
| Dai Wong: | Fifth Palace – "The Peak" |
| Ding: | The fourth of the Heavenly Stems, signifying Yang Fire |
| Dung: | Winter |
| Feng Shui: | Wind (and) Water |
| Fin Kams: | An inner ring of the luo p'an – "120 pieces of gold". |
| Fiu Gong: | San Sat, the sign of a gambler |
| Fun: | Equinox |
| Gan Zi: | Stem/Branch – the Cycle of Sixty Stems and |

| | |
|---|---|
| | Branches |
| Gap: | Cantonese for first (yang Wood) Stem (= chia/ jia) |
| Gay: | (=ji) Cantonese for the sixth (Yin Earth) Stem |
| Gee: | Solstice |
| Geng: | Theseventh (Yang Metal) Stem |
| Gip Choi: | Sap San – "Rob Wealth" |
| Gip Sat: | San Sat – "Robbery and Disaster" |
| Goo San: | San Sat relating to relationship |
| Gui: | (= quai) tenth (Yin Water) Stem. Can be "ghost", also Hexagram 38 |
| Gung: | See "geng" above |
| Gung Hei Fat Choi: | New Year Greeting – wishing wealth and abundance |
| Ha: | Summer |
| Hai: | Mandarin: astrological Pig |
| Hohn: | Cold |
| Hoi: | Cantonese – astrological Pig |
| Hong Yim: | Sat San Sat – nascent relationship issues |
| Hung Mo: | Dead and Empty, Void – applied among other things to Palaces |
| Hung Mo Yan: | Void Resource |
| Jee: | Cantonese: astrological Snake |
| Jeung Sing: | San Sat: won't be second-best |
| Ji: | Cantonese (= gay) sixth (Yin Water) Stem |
| Jing: | Sap Sans – Direct/Opposite Polarity |
| Jing Choi: | Sap San – Direct Wealth |
| Jing Kun: | Sap San – Direct Officer (Direct Challenge) |
| Jing Yan: | Sap San – Direct Resource |
| Koon Tai: | Third Palace – Ascending – education |
| Kua: | "Image"; typically Trigrams or Hexagrams (Dai Kua=Da Gua) |
| Kun: | Sap San meaning Challenge, Power and Discipline |

| | |
|---|---|
| Kun/Choi: | A productive relationship (e.g., marriage), but also a Clash |
| Lap Yum: | An Inner ring of the Luo P'an – The 72 Dragons |
| Lo Shu: | 9-box "Magic" square |
| Loy Hong Yim Sat: | San Sat – Serious relationship issues |
| Lum Kun: | Fourth Palace – Education and Qualification |
| Luo P'an: | Chinese Compass |
| Mao: | Ninth Palace: The Vault |
| Man Cheung: | San Sat – Adult Education |
| May: | Eighth Branch Cantonese (=Wei) astrological Sheep |
| Mo Chi: | The Great Singularity before Creation |
| Mo Yuk: | Second Palace: Filthy Water |
| Mong San: | San Sat – averse to one or other Element and polarity |
| Mow: | Fourth Branch – the astrological Rabbit |
| Mun: | Increase; as in Siu Mun, Small Increase |
| Muw: | See "Mow" above. |
| Ng: | Cantonese – Seventh Branch: the astrological Horse |
| Pin: | Sap San – Indirect/same polarity |
| Pin Choi: | Sap Sans – Indirect (unearned) Wealth |
| Pin Kun: | Sap Sans – Indirect Challenge |
| Pin Yan: | Sap Sans – Indirect Resource |
| Por Kwan: | Jiu shape relating Yin Metal – Broken Soldier |
| Qing: | Affection |
| Qua Suk: | San Sat – withdrawal from relationship |
| Quai: | (= gui) tenth (Yin Water) Stem. Can be "ghost" also Hexagram 38 |
| Ren: | (= yum) Cantonese: ninth (Yang Water) Stem |
| Sai: | Eighth Palace – Death (rarely literal) |
| Sam He Feng Shui: | Or Yang Gong – Three Harmony feng shui – "Ba Zi on the ground" |

| | |
|---|---|
| San Sats: | Special Stars |
| Sap Gon Luk | San Sat: success through education |
| Sap Sans: | Ten characters representing the relationship of all the characters of a Ba Zi with the Day Stem |
| Shen: | Ninth Branch astrological Monkey |
| Shua: | Sixth Palace: Past the Peak |
| Shu: | Heat |
| Si: | Mandarin – Sixth Branch astrological Snake (= jee) |
| Siu: | Cantonese – Small (= Hsiao) |
| Shun: | Cantonese fifth Branch, the astrological Dragon (= Zhen) |
| Shuut: | Snow |
| Sik Sun: | Sap San – Eating God, Direct Output |
| Soi: | Mandarin – Water |
| Su: | Mandarin – Eleventh Branch astrological Dog (= sute) |
| Sute: | Cantonese – Eleventh Branch astrological Dog (= su) |
| Tai yang: | The Greater Yang – bigram |
| Tai yin: | The Greater Yin – bigram |
| Tao Te Ching: | of Lao Tze – the founding volume of Taoist thought |
| Tin Duk: | San Sat – Heavenly Blessing |
| Tin Yute Gwai Yan: | San Sat – Noble Friend, Mentor |
| Toe Far: | Irresistible; characters at the Cardinal Compass Points |
| Toi: | Eleventh Palace – Pregnant |
| Tsun: | Eighth (Yin Metal) Stem |
| Tze: | Mandarin for the Cantonese "chee", meaning the astrological Rat, the first of the Branches in the daily sequence |
| Wah Koi: | San Sat – Princess, clever but lonely |

Wei: Eighth Branch Mandarin (= May) astrological Sheep

Wu: Seventh Branch Mandarin (= Ng) astrological Horse. Also "not" as in "wu wei" not doing; also "five"

Wu Xing: Five Elements or Stages

Xiao Yang: Bigram: Lesser Yang

Xiao Yin: Bigram: Lesser Yin

Xuan Kong Da Gua: Literally "Mystery of the Void" – Hexagram feng shui

Yang: As opposed to Yin, something like the masculine principle

Yan: Sap San – Resource

Yeung Yan: San Sat – Goat Blade, haste, poor timing

Yi: One

Yik Ma: San Sat – the Racehorse Star

Yin: As opposed to Yang, something like the feminine principle

Yu: Rain

Yum: (= Ren) Cantonese – Ninth (Yang Water) Stem

Yum San: Cantonese (= Yuan Zhen) – the Unbonded Star

Yung: Quickening

Yute: (= Yi) Cantonese – second (Yin Wood) Stem Also, "Moon"

Yute Duk: San Sat – Blessings of the Moon

Yute Yeung: San Sat – Monthly Leader

Yuw: Tenth Earthly Branch; astrological Rooster

Zeun Kun: Sap San – Indirect Output, Hurting Officer

Zhen: Fifth Branch; astrological Dragon; also "Thunder"

Zhou Yi: The *Book of Changes* or *Yi*

# Tables for Calculation and Drafting

| *Mr. or Ms.* | ***Elements Request*** | ***Life House*** | ***Time*** | ***Day*** | ***Month*** | ***Year*** | ***Male Or Female*** |
|---|---|---|---|---|---|---|---|
| | | | | | | | ***Sap San*** |
| | | | | | | | ***5 Element*** |
| | | | | | | | ***Stems*** |
| | | | | | | | ***Branches*** |
| | | | | | | | ***5 Element*** |
| | | | | | | | ***Yin or Yang*** |
| | ***Elements to Avoid*** | | | | | | ***Hidden Stems*** |
| | | | | | | | ***Sap San*** |
| | | | | | | | ***12 Palace*** |
| | | | | | | | ***Empty Palace*** |
| | | | | | | | ***San Sat*** |

| | | | | | | |
|---|---|---|---|---|---|---|
| : | : | : | : | : | : | *Date* |
| | | | | | | *Big Fate Stems* |
| | | | | | | *Current Year Fate* |
| | | | | | | |
| | | | | | | |
| | | | | | | |
| | | | | | | |
| | | | | | | |

| | | | | | | |
|---|---|---|---|---|---|---|
| : | : | : | : | : | : | *Date* |
| | | | | | | *Big Fate Branches* |
| | | | | | | *Current Year Fate* |
| | | | | | | |
| | | | | | | |
| | | | | | | |
| | | | | | | |
| | | | | | | |
| | | | | | | **Palace San Sat** |

## The Cycles of Change 1™

| | | | | Rats |
|---|---|---|---|---|
| 壬子 | 庚子 | 戊子 | 丙子 | 甲子 |
| **Mulberry Tree** | **Earthen Walls** | **Lightning Fire** | **Channeled Water** | **Gold from the Sea** |
| Spiritual Gifts, More fragile than they look. | Dry, brittle Easily broken. | Short fuse. Melts metal but wood resists. | Underground water strong, steady, Inscrutable. | Can't cut wood Deep and reserved. |
| **1E or 8W** | **4E or 2W** | **1E or 8W** | **4E or 2W** | **7W or 8W** |
| *The Rat on the Mountain* | *The Rat on the Beam* | *The Rat in the Warehouse* | *The Rat in the Field* | *The Rat on the Roof* |
| **1972** | **1960** | **2008** | **1996** | **1984** |
| 8 | 2 | 7 | 6 | 1 |
| 1 | 9 | 4 | 3 | 8 |

| | | | | Oxen |
|---|---|---|---|---|
| 癸丑 | 辛丑 | 己丑 | 丁丑 | 乙丑 |
| **Mulberry Tree** | **Earthen Walls** | **Lightning Fire** | **Channeled Water** | **Gold from the Sea** |
| Spiritual Gifts, More fragile than they look. | Busy, busy, busy Emotional. | Short fuse. Melts metal but wood resists. | Underground water strong, steady, Inscrutable. | Can't cut wood Deep and reserved. |
| **9E or 6W** | **3E** | **9E or 6W** | **3E** | **6W or 9E** |
| *The Ox outside the Gate* | *The Ox on the Way* | *The Ox inside the Gate* | *The Ox in the Lake* | *The Ox in the Sea* |
| **1973** | **1961** | **2009** | **1997** | **1985** |
| 6 | 1 | 9 | 4 | 3 |
| 8 | 3 | 2 | 7 | 6 |

| | | | | Tigers |
|---|---|---|---|---|
| 甲寅 | 壬寅 | 庚寅 | 戊寅 | 丙寅 |
| **Big Stream Water** | **Gold Foil** | **Pine Tree** | **Rampart Earth** | **Furnace Fire** |
| Busy, busy, busy Emotional | Weak, flashy insubstantial. | Reliable, solid, Team player. | Strong outside, Weak inside | Strong, warm Can melt metal. |
| **8W or 7W** | **2W or 4E** | **8W or 7W** | **2W or 4E** | **2W or 1E** |
| *The Tiger Standing Still* | *The Tiger passing through the Forest* | *The Tiger going down the Mountain* | *The Tiger passing through the Mountain* | *The Tiger in the Forest* |
| **1974** | **1962** | **2010** | **1998** | **1986** |
| 7 | 9 | 3 (4 | 8 | 2 |
| 9 | 7 | 1 2] | 6 | 4 |

## The Cycles of Change 2™

| | | | | Rabbits |
|---|---|---|---|---|
| 乙卯 | 癸卯 | 辛卯 | 己卯 | 丁卯 |
| **Big Stream Water** | **Gold Foil** | **Pine Tree** | **Rampart Earth** | **Furnace Fire** |
| **Busy, busy, busy Emotional** | **Weak, flashy insubstantial.** | **Reliable, solid, Team player.** | **Strong outside, Weak inside** | **Strong, warm Can melt metal.** |
| **7W or 8W** | **1E or 8W** | **7W or 8W** | **1E or 8W** | **4E or 2W** |
| *The Buddha Rabbit* | *Rabbit running in the Forest* | *The Rabbit in the Burrow* | *Rabbit running out of the Forest* | *Rabbit looking at the Moon* |
| **1975** | **1963** | **2011** | **1999** | **1987** |
| **1** | **8** | **2** | **7** | **6** |
| **4** | **7** | **3** | **8** | **9** |

| | | | | Dragons |
|---|---|---|---|---|
| 丙辰 | 甲辰 | 壬辰 | 庚辰 | 戊辰 |
| **Gravelly Earth** | **Candle Flame** | **Long Flowing Water** | **White Wax Metal** | **Forest Tree** |
| **Industrious but dispersed. Mixed chi, lots of ideas.** | **Light in the dark, low profile, easily Discouraged.** | **Steadfast, the best at relationship** | **Literally insincere: Can't cut wood, Easily melted by fire.** | **Strong, stable, trustworthy, avoid Lightning Fire. Takes double metal to cut.** |
| **6W or 9E** | **9E or 6W** | **6W or 9E** | **9E or 6W** | **3E** |
| *Dragon Flying to Heaven.* | *The Cheerful Dragon* | *Dragon in the Rain.* | *Angry Dragon* | *Yielding Dragon* |
| **1976** | **1964** | **2012** | **2000** | **1988** |
| **4** | **3** | **6** | **1** | **9** |
| **1** | **2** | **4** | **9** | **6** |

| | | | | Snakes |
|---|---|---|---|---|
| 丁巳 | 乙巳 | 癸巳 | 辛巳 | 己巳 |
| **Gravelly Earth** | **Candle Flame** | **Long Flowing Water** | **White Wax Metal** | **Forest Tree** |
| **2W or 1E** | **8W or 7W** | **2W or 4E** | **8W or 7W** | **2E or 4E** |
| **Industrious but dispersed. Mixed chi, lots of ideas.** | **Light in the dark, low profile, easily Discouraged.** | **Steadfast, the best at relationship** | **Literally insincere: Can't cut wood, Easily melted by. by fire** | **Strong, stable, trustworthy, avoid Lightning Fire. Takes double metal to cut.** |
| *Snake in the Fish Pond* | *Snake coming out of the hole* | *The Snake on the Grass* | *Snake Sleeping in Winter* | *The Prosperous Snake* |
| **1977** | **1965** | **1953** | **2001** | **1989** |
| **2** | **7** | **4** | **3** | **8** |
| **8** | **3** | **6** | **7** | **2** |

## The Cycles of Change 3™

| | | | | Horses |
|---|---|---|---|---|
| 戊午 | 丙午 | 甲午 | 壬午 | 庚午 |
| **Heavenly Fire** | **Celestial River** | **Metal in the Sand** | **Willow Tree** | **Soil lies on the Road** |
| **Sky Fire, can't melt metal. Flexible, open and adaptable.** | **Rain from heaven. Traveller Communicator** | **Industrious inventive Hard to read.** | **Followers cut by metal Hangers on** | **Butterfly mind. Doesn't complete.** |
| **4E or 2W** | **7W or 8W** | **1E or 8W** | **7W or 8W** | **1E or 8W** |
| *Horse within the Gate* | *Horse on the Way* | *Horse in the Clouds* | *Horse in the Army* | *Horse in the Hall.* |
| **1978** | **1966** | **1954** | **2002** | **1990** |
| $\frac{3}{4}$ | $\frac{4}{3}$ | $\frac{9}{1}$ | $\frac{2}{1}$ | $\frac{8}{9}$ |

| | | | | Sheep |
|---|---|---|---|---|
| 己未 | 丁未 | 乙未 | 癸未 | 辛未 |
| **Heavenly Fire** | **Celestial River** | **Metal in the Sand** | **Willow Tree** | **Soil lies on the Road** |
| **Sky Fire, can't melt metal. Flexible, open and adaptable.** | **Rain from heaven. Traveller Communicator** | **Industrious inventive Hard to read.** | **Followers cut by metal Hangers on** | **Butterfly mind. Doesn't complete.** |
| **3E** | **6W or 9E** | **9E or 6W** | **6W or 9E** | **9E or 6W** |
| *Sheep running on the Mountain* | *The Lonely Sheep* | *Sheep respected by others* | *Sheep in the Flock* | *Prosperous Sheep* |
| **1979** | **1967** | **1955** | **2003** | **1991** |
| $\frac{1}{2}$ | $\frac{6}{7}$ | $\frac{7}{6}$ | $\frac{4}{8}$ | $\frac{9}{3}$ |

| | | | Monkeys | |
|---|---|---|---|---|
| 庚申 | 戊申 | 丙申 | 甲申 | 壬申 |
| **Pomegranate Wood** | **Roadway Earth** | **Fire under Mountain** | **Spring Water** | **Sword Edge Metal** |
| **Hard exterior, soft centre.Deceptive, bluffer.** | **Strong, stubborn, predictable. Can't withstand Forest Tree** | **Will blow! Passionate and reserved.** | **Fresh, original, inventive and generous.** | **Strong, fair and razor sharp.** |
| **2W or 4E** | **2W or 1E** | **8W or 7W** | **2W or 1E** | **8W or 7W** |
| *Monkey in a Fruit Tree* | *Lonely Monkey* | *Monkey climbing up the Mountain* | *Monkey climbing a Tree* | *The Elegant Monkey* |
| **1980** | **1968** | **1956** | **2004** | **1992** |
| $\frac{7}{1}$ | $\frac{2}{6}$ | $\frac{8}{4}$ | $\frac{3}{9}$ | $\frac{1}{7}$ |

# The Cycles of Change 4™

| | | | | Roosters |
|---|---|---|---|---|
| 辛酉 | 己酉 | 丁酉 | 乙酉 | 癸酉 |
| **Pomegranate Wood** | **Roadway Earth** | **Fire under Mountain** | **Spring Water** | **Sword Edge Metal** |
| **Hard exterior, soft centre.Deceptive, bluffer.** | **Strong, stubborn, predictable. Can't withstand Forest Tree** | **Will blow! Passionate and reserved.** | **Fresh, original, inventive and generous.** | **Strong, fair and razor sharp.** |
| **1E or 8W** | **4E or 9E** | **7W or 8W** | **4E or 2W** | **7W or 8W** |
| *Rooster in a Cage* | *Rooster announcing Dawn* | *Lonely Rooster* | *Singing Rooster* | *Rooster in the Hen Roost* |
| **1981** | **1969** | **1957** | **2005** | **1993** |
| 8 | 3 | 4 | 9 | 2 |
| 3 | 8 | 9 | 4 | 7 |

| | | | | Dogs |
|---|---|---|---|---|
| 壬戌 | 庚戌 | 戊戌 | 丙戌 | 甲戌 |
| **Ocean Water** | **Double Edged Sword** | **Bushes & Trees on the Plain** | **Roofing Slates** | **Beacon Fire** |
| **Avoid for Earth position and Fire Site.Deep, wise, Knowledgable** | **Two-faced. Avoid wood here. Avoid door here.** | **Loners and introverts** | **Sincere but not as protective as they want to be Overcommitted.** | **Good at communicat-ion if interested** |
| **9E or 6W** | **3E** | **6W or 9E** | **3E** | **6W or 9E** |
| *Family Dog* | *Temple Dog* | *Dog going into the Mountain* | *Sleepy Dog* | *Dog on Guard* |
| **1982** | **1970** | **1958** | **2006** | **1994** |
| 4 | 9 | 1 | 6 | 7 |
| 4 | 9 | 6 | 1 | 2 |

| | | | | Pigs |
|---|---|---|---|---|
| 癸亥 | 辛亥 | 己亥 | 丁亥 | 乙亥 |
| **Ocean Water** | **Double Edged Sword** | **Bushes & Trees on the Plain** | **Roofing Slates** | **Beacon Fire** |
| **Avoid for Earth position and Fire Site.Deep, wise, Knowledgable** | **Two-faced. Avoid wood here. Avoid door here.** | **Loners and introverts** | **Sincere but not as protective as they want to be** | **Good at communicat-ion if** |
| **8W or 7W** | **2W or 4E** | **2W or 1E** | **2E or 4E** | **2W or 1E** |
| *Pig in the Forest* | *Pig in the Garden* | *Monastery Pig* | *Pig passing the Mountain* | *Pig passing by* |
| **1983** | **1971** | **1959** | **2007** | **1995** |
| 6 | 7 | 2 | 8 | 3 |
| 6 | 7 | 2 | 8 | 3 |

**HOUR BRANCHES** →

| 'New' Month Branch ('New' if Day Pillar in 2nd Solar Fortnight) ↓ | | 辰 | 巳 | 午 | 未 | 申 | 酉 | 戌 | 亥 | 子 | 丑 | 寅 | 卯 |
|---|---|---|---|---|---|---|---|---|---|---|---|---|---|
| | 寅 | 亥 | 戌 | 酉 | 申 | 未 | 午 | 巳 | 辰 | 卯 | 寅 | 丑 | 子 |
| | 卯 | 戌 | 酉 | 申 | 未 | 午 | 巳 | 辰 | 卯 | 寅 | 丑 | 子 | 亥 |
| | 辰 | 酉 | 申 | 未 | 午 | 巳 | 辰 | 卯 | 寅 | 丑 | 子 | 亥 | 戌 |
| | 巳 | 申 | 未 | 午 | 巳 | 辰 | 卯 | 寅 | 丑 | 子 | 亥 | 戌 | 酉 |
| | 午 | 未 | 午 | 巳 | 辰 | 卯 | 寅 | 丑 | 子 | 亥 | 戌 | 酉 | 申 |
| | 未 | 午 | 巳 | 辰 | 卯 | 寅 | 丑 | 子 | 亥 | 戌 | 酉 | 申 | 未 |
| | 申 | 巳 | 辰 | 卯 | 寅 | 丑 | 子 | 亥 | 戌 | 酉 | 申 | 未 | 午 |
| | 酉 | 辰 | 卯 | 寅 | 丑 | 子 | 亥 | 戌 | 酉 | 申 | 未 | 午 | 巳 |
| | 戌 | 卯 | 寅 | 丑 | 子 | 亥 | 戌 | 酉 | 申 | 未 | 午 | 巳 | 辰 |
| | 亥 | 寅 | 丑 | 子 | 亥 | 戌 | 酉 | 申 | 未 | 午 | 巳 | 辰 | 卯 |
| | 子 | 丑 | 子 | 亥 | 戌 | 酉 | 申 | 未 | 午 | 巳 | 辰 | 卯 | 寅 |
| | 丑 | 子 | 亥 | 戌 | 酉 | 申 | 未 | 午 | 巳 | 辰 | 卯 | 寅 | 丑 |

**LIFE HOUSE BRANCH FINDER**

**HIDDEN STEMS**

| December<br>子<br>Rat | January<br>丑<br>Ox | February<br>寅<br>Tiger | March<br>卯<br>Rabbit | April<br>辰<br>Dragon | May<br>巳<br>Snake | June<br>午<br>Horse | July<br>未<br>Sheep | August<br>申<br>Monkey | September<br>酉<br>Rooster | October<br>戌<br>Dog | November<br>亥<br>Pig |
|---|---|---|---|---|---|---|---|---|---|---|---|
| Yum/Ren<br>壬 (10)<br>Yang Water | Quai<br>癸 (9)<br>Yin Water | Mow/Wu<br>戊 (7)<br>Yang Earth | Gap/Chia<br>甲(10)<br>Yang Wood | Yute/Yi<br>乙(9)<br>Yin Wood | Mow/Wu<br>戊(5)<br>Yang Earth | Bing<br>丙(10)<br>Yang Fire | Ding<br>丁(9)<br>Yin Fire | Gay/Ji<br>Mow/wu<br>戊 己(10) | Geng<br>庚(10)<br>Yang Metal | Tsun<br>辛(9)<br>Yin Metal | Mow/Wu<br>戊(7)<br>Yang Earth |
| | Tsun<br>辛 (3)<br>Yin Metal | Bing<br>丙 (7)<br>Yang Fire | | Quai<br>癸 (3)<br>Yin Water | Geng<br>庚 (9)<br>Yang Metal | Gay/Ji<br>己 (9)<br>Yin Earth | Yute/Yi<br>乙 (3)<br>Yin Wood | Ren<br>壬 (3)<br>Yang Water | | Ding<br>丁 (3)<br>Yin Fire | Gap/Chia<br>甲 (5)<br>Yang Wood |
| Quai<br>癸 (20)<br>Yin Water | Gay/Ji<br>己 (18)<br>Yin Earth | Gap/Chia<br>甲 (16)<br>Yang Wood | Yute/Yi<br>乙 (20)<br>Yin Wood | Mow/Wu<br>戊 (18)<br>Yang Earth | Bing<br>丙 (16)<br>Yang Fire | Ding<br>丁 (11)<br>Yin Fire | Gay/Ji<br>己 (18)<br>Yin Earth | Yum/Ren<br>戊 (17)<br>Yang Metal<br>Geng | Tsun<br>辛 (20)<br>Yin Metal | Mow Wu<br>戊 (18)<br>Yang Earth | Yum/Ren<br>壬 (18)<br>Yang Water |

| FINDING THE PALACES | | | | | | | | | | | |
|---|---|---|---|---|---|---|---|---|---|---|---|
| | STEMS | 癸 | 壬 | 辛 | 庚 | 己 | 戊 | 丁 | 丙 | 乙 | 甲 | |
| BRANCHES | | 卯 | 申 | 子 | 巳 | 酉 | 寅 | 酉 | 寅 | 午 | 亥 | Chang Sang |
| | | 寅 | 酉 | 亥 | 午 | 申 | 卯 | 申 | 卯 | 巳 | 子 | Mo Yuk |
| | | 丑 | 戌 | 戌 | 未 | 未 | 辰 | 未 | 辰 | 辰 | 丑 | Koon Tai |
| | | 子 | 亥 | 酉 | 申 | 午 | 巳 | 午 | 巳 | 卯 | 寅 | Lum Kun |
| | | 亥 | 子 | 申 | 酉 | 巳 | 午 | 巳 | 午 | 寅 | 卯 | Dai Wong |
| | | 戌 | 丑 | 未 | 戌 | 辰 | 未 | 辰 | 未 | 丑 | 辰 | Shua |
| | | 酉 | 寅 | 午 | 亥 | 卯 | 申 | 卯 | 申 | 子 | 巳 | Bang |
| | | 申 | 卯 | 巳 | 子 | 寅 | 酉 | 寅 | 酉 | 亥 | 午 | Sai |
| | | 未 | 辰 | 辰 | 丑 | 丑 | 戌 | 丑 | 戌 | 戌 | 未 | Mao |
| | | 午 | 巳 | 卯 | 寅 | 子 | 亥 | 子 | 亥 | 酉 | 申 | Chua |
| | | 巳 | 午 | 寅 | 卯 | 亥 | 子 | 亥 | 子 | 申 | 酉 | Toi |
| | | 辰 | 未 | 丑 | 辰 | 戌 | 丑 | 戌 | 丑 | 未 | 戌 | Yung |

**FINDING THE EMPTY PALACES**

| | | | | | |
|---|---|---|---|---|---|
| 寅甲 | 辰甲 | 午甲 | 申甲 | 戌甲 | 子甲 |
| 卯乙 | 巳乙 | 未乙 | 酉乙 | 亥乙 | 丑乙 |
| 辰丙 | 午丙 | 申丙 | 戌丙 | 子丙 | 寅丙 |
| 巳丁 | 未丁 | 酉丁 | 亥丁 | 丑丁 | 寅丁 |
| 午戊 | 申戊 | 戌戊 | 子戊 | 寅戊 | 辰戊 |
| 未己 | 酉己 | 亥己 | 丑己 | 卯己 | 巳己 |
| 申庚 | 戌庚 | 子庚 | 寅庚 | 辰庚 | 午庚 |
| 酉辛 | 亥辛 | 丑辛 | 卯辛 | 巳辛 | 未辛 |
| 戌壬 | 子壬 | 寅壬 | 辰壬 | 午壬 | 申壬 |
| 亥癸 | 丑癸 | 卯癸 | 巳癸 | 未癸 | 酉癸 |
| 子丑 | 寅卯 | 辰巳 | 午未 | 申酉 | 戌亥 |

SAP SAN Indications:
Empty Bay Gin/Gip Choi: No benefit from siblings.
Empty Sik Sun/Zeun Kun: No benefit from children.
Empty Jing Choi/Pin Choi: Reduce wealth.
Empty Jing Kun/Pin Kun: Reduce power and influence.
Empty Jing Yan/Pin Yan: No benefit from parents.

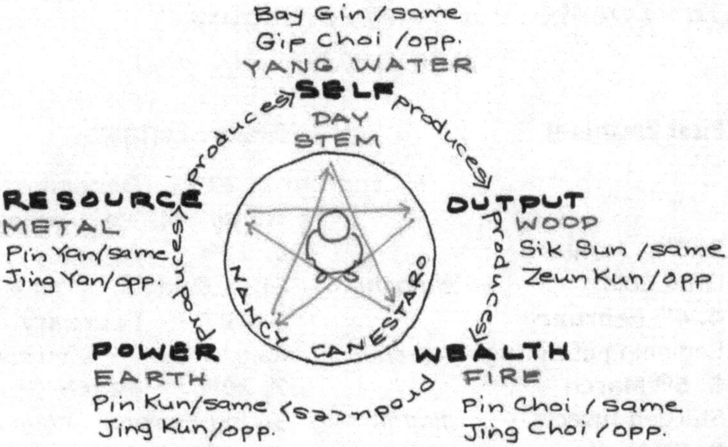


DAY STEM 壬 REN, YANG WATER

**SAP SANS / TEN GODS**

| | LIFE HOUSE | TIME | DAY | MONTH | YEAR |
|---|---|---|---|---|---|
| POLARITY | YIN | YANG | YANG | YANG | YIN |
| 5-ELEM. | EARTH | FIRE | WATER | WATER | FIRE |
| STEM | 己 | 丙 | 壬 | 壬 | 丁 |
| STEM | JI | BING | REN | REN | DING |
| | | | | | |
| ANIMAL | ROOSTER | HORSE | DOG | TIGER | PIG |
| BRANCH | YOU | WU | XU | YIN | HAI |
| BRANCH | 酉 | 午 | 戌 | 寅 | 亥 |
| 5-ELEM. | METAL | FIRE | EARTH | WOOD | WATER |
| POLARITY | YIN | YANG | YANG | YANG | YIN |

# The Twenty Four Solar Fortnights.

| First Fortnight | | Second Fortnight | |
|---|---|---|---|
| | 1°Capricorn | **1. 22nd December** | |
| | | Winter Solstice | *dung gee* |
| **2. 5th January** | | **3. 20th January** | |
| Little Cold | *siu hohn* | Great Cold | *dai hohn* |
| **4. 4th February** | | **5. 19th February** | |
| Beginning of Spring | *lap chun* | Rain Water | *yu soi* |
| **6. 5th March** | | **7. 20th March** | |
| Startled Insects | *ging jit* | Spring Equinox | *chun fun* |
| **8. 5th April** | | **9. 20th April** | |
| Great Brightness | *ching ming* | Grain Rains | *kuk yu* |
| **10. 5th May** | | **11. 21st May** | |
| Beginning of Summer | *lap ha* | Small Increase | *siu mun* |
| **12. 6th June** | | **13. 21st June** | |
| Grain in Ear | *mong chun* | Summer Solstice | *ha gee* |
| **14. 7th July** | | **15. 23rd July** | |
| Little Heat | *siu shu* | Great Heat | *dai shu* |
| **16. 7th August** | | **17. 23rd August** | |
| Beginning of Autumn | *lap chow* | Limit of Heat | *chu shu* |
| **18. 7th September** | | **19.23rd September** | |
| White Dew | *bak lo* | Autumn Equinox | *chow fun* |
| **20. 8th October** | | **21. 23rd October** | |
| Cold Dew | *hohn lo* | Frost Descends | *zeun gong* |
| **22. 7th November** | | **23. 22nd November** | |
| Beginning of Winter | *lap dung* | Little Snow | *siu shuut* |
| **24. 7th December** | | | |
| Great Snow | *dai shuut* | | |

**TIGERS CHASING**

| 戊<br>癸 | 丁<br>壬 | 丙<br>辛 | 乙<br>庚 | 甲<br>己 | STEM / BRANCH |
|---|---|---|---|---|---|
| 寅甲 | 寅壬 | 寅庚 | 寅戊 | 寅丙 | 寅 |
| 卯乙 | 卯癸 | 卯辛 | 卯己 | 卯丁 | 卯 |
| 辰丙 | 辰甲 | 辰壬 | 辰庚 | 辰戊 | 辰 |
| 巳丁 | 巳乙 | 巳癸 | 巳辛 | 巳己 | 巳 |
| 午戊 | 午酉 | 午甲 | 午壬 | 午庚 | 午 |
| 未己 | 未丁 | 未乙 | 未癸 | 未辛 | 未 |
| 申庚 | 申戊 | 申丙 | 申甲 | 申壬 | 申 |
| 酉辛 | 酉己 | 酉丁 | 酉乙 | 酉癸 | 酉 |
| 戌壬 | 戌庚 | 戌戊 | 戌丙 | 戌甲 | 戌 |
| 亥癸 | 亥辛 | 亥己 | 亥丁 | 亥乙 | 亥 |
| 子甲 | 子壬 | 子庚 | 子戊 | 子丙 | 子 |
| 丑乙 | 丑癸 | 丑辛 | 丑己 | 丑丁 | 丑 |

**RATS CHASING THE HOUR**

| 戊<br>癸 | 丁<br>壬 | 丙<br>辛 | 乙<br>庚 | 甲<br>己 | STEM / BRANCH |
|---|---|---|---|---|---|
| 子壬 | 子庚 | 子戊 | 子丙 | 子甲 | 子 |
| 丑癸 | 丑辛 | 丑己 | 丑丁 | 丑乙 | 丑 |
| 寅甲 | 寅壬 | 寅庚 | 寅戊 | 寅丙 | 寅 |
| 卯乙 | 卯癸 | 卯辛 | 卯己 | 卯丁 | 卯 |
| 辰丙 | 辰甲 | 辰壬 | 辰庚 | 辰戊 | 辰 |
| 巳丁 | 巳乙 | 巳癸 | 巳辛 | 巳己 | 巳 |
| 午戊 | 午酉 | 午甲 | 午壬 | 午庚 | 午 |
| 未己 | 未丁 | 未乙 | 未癸 | 未辛 | 未 |
| 申庚 | 申戊 | 申丙 | 申甲 | 申壬 | 申 |
| 酉辛 | 酉己 | 酉丁 | 酉乙 | 酉癸 | 酉 |
| 戌壬 | 戌庚 | 戌戊 | 戌丙 | 戌甲 | 戌 |
| 亥癸 | 亥辛 | 亥己 | 亥丁 | 亥乙 | 亥 |

| 公曆 CE 2023 2023 - 2024 | 癸 卯 Gui Mao | 兔 Year of Rabbit | 納音五行 金箔金 值年宿 井木犴 |
|---|---|---|---|

| 陰曆月 | 正月小 | 二月大 | 閏二月 | 三月小 | 四月大 | 五月大 |
|---|---|---|---|---|---|---|
| 陽曆月 | 甲寅 | 乙卯 | | 丙辰 | 丁巳 | 戊午 |
| 月紫白 | 8 | 7 | | 6 | 5 | 4 |
| 節氣 | 立春 1 10:42 | 驚蟄 3 4:36 | 清明 5 9:13 | | | |
| | 雨水 2 6:34 | 春分 4 5:24 | | 穀雨 6 16:14 | 小滿 8 15:09 | 夏至 10 22:58 |
| | | | | 立夏 7 2:19 | 芒種 9 6:18 | 小暑 11 16:31 |
| 初一 | 1/22 庚辰 | 2/20 己酉 | 3/22 己卯 | 4/20 戊申 | 5/19 丁丑 | 6/18 丁未 |
| 初二 | 1/23 辛巳 | 2/21 庚戌 | 3/23 庚辰 | 4/21 己酉 | 5/20 戊寅 | 6/19 戊申 |
| 初三 | 1/24 壬午 | 2/22 辛亥 | 3/24 辛巳 | 4/22 庚戌 | 5/21 己卯 | 6/20 己酉 |
| 初四 | 1/25 癸未 | 2/23 壬子 | 3/25 壬午 | 4/23 辛亥 | 5/22 庚辰 | 6/21 庚戌 |
| 初五 | 1/26 甲申 | 2/24 癸丑 | 3/26 癸未 | 4/24 壬子 | 5/23 辛巳 | 6/22 辛亥 |
| 初六 | 1/27 乙酉 | 2/25 甲寅 | 3/27 甲申 | 4/25 癸丑 | 5/24 壬午 | 6/23 壬子 |
| 初七 | 1/28 丙戌 | 2/26 乙卯 | 3/28 乙酉 | 4/26 甲寅 | 5/25 癸未 | 6/24 癸丑 |
| 初八 | 1/29 丁亥 | 2/27 丙辰 | 3/29 丙戌 | 4/27 乙卯 | 5/26 甲申 | 6/25 甲寅 |
| 初九 | 1/30 戊子 | 2/28 丁巳 | 3/30 丁亥 | 4/28 丙辰 | 5/27 乙酉 | 6/26 乙卯 |
| 初十 | 1/31 己丑 | 3/1 戊午 | 3/31 戊子 | 4/29 丁巳 | 5/28 丙戌 | 6/27 丙辰 |
| 十一 | 2/1 庚寅 | 3/2 己未 | 4/1 己丑 | 4/30 戊午 | 5/29 丁亥 | 6/28 丁巳 |
| 十二 | 2/2 辛卯 | 3/3 庚申 | 4/2 庚寅 | 5/1 己未 | 5/30 戊子 | 6/29 戊午 |
| 十三 | 2/3 壬辰 | 3/4 辛酉 | 4/3 辛卯 | 5/2 庚申 | 5/31 己丑 | 6/30 己未 |
| 十四 | 2/4 癸巳 | 3/5 壬戌 | 4/4 壬辰 | 5/3 辛酉 | 6/1 庚寅 | 7/1 庚申 |
| 十五 | 2/5 甲午 | 3/6 癸亥 | 4/5 癸巳 | 5/4 壬戌 | 6/2 辛卯 | 7/2 辛酉 |
| 十六 | 2/6 乙未 | 3/7 甲子 | 4/6 甲午 | 5/5 癸亥 | 6/3 壬辰 | 7/3 壬戌 |
| 十七 | 2/7 丙申 | 3/8 乙丑 | 4/7 乙未 | 5/6 甲子 | 6/4 癸巳 | 7/4 癸亥 |
| 十八 | 2/8 丁酉 | 3/9 丙寅 | 4/8 丙申 | 5/7 乙丑 | 6/5 甲午 | 7/5 甲子 |
| 十九 | 2/9 戊戌 | 3/10 丁卯 | 4/9 丁酉 | 5/8 丙寅 | 6/6 乙未 | 7/6 乙丑 |
| 二十 | 2/10 己亥 | 3/11 戊辰 | 4/10 戊戌 | 5/9 丁卯 | 6/7 丙申 | 7/7 丙寅 |
| 廿一 | 2/11 庚子 | 3/12 己巳 | 4/11 己亥 | 5/10 戊辰 | 6/8 丁酉 | 7/8 丁卯 |
| 廿二 | 2/12 辛丑 | 3/13 庚午 | 4/12 庚子 | 5/11 己巳 | 6/9 戊戌 | 7/9 戊辰 |
| 廿三 | 2/13 壬寅 | 3/14 辛未 | 4/13 辛丑 | 5/12 庚午 | 6/10 己亥 | 7/10 己巳 |
| 廿四 | 2/14 癸卯 | 3/15 壬申 | 4/14 壬寅 | 5/13 辛未 | 6/11 庚子 | 7/11 庚午 |
| 廿五 | 2/15 甲辰 | 3/16 癸酉 | 4/15 癸卯 | 5/14 壬申 | 6/12 辛丑 | 7/12 辛未 |
| 廿六 | 2/16 乙巳 | 3/17 甲戌 | 4/16 甲辰 | 5/15 癸酉 | 6/13 壬寅 | 7/13 壬申 |
| 廿七 | 2/17 丙午 | 3/18 乙亥 | 4/17 乙巳 | 5/16 甲戌 | 6/14 癸卯 | 7/14 癸酉 |
| 廿八 | 2/18 丁未 | 3/19 丙子 | 4/18 丙午 | 5/17 乙亥 | 6/15 甲辰 | 7/15 甲戌 |
| 廿九 | 2/19 戊申 | 3/20 丁丑 | 4/19 丁未 | 5/18 丙子 | 6/16 乙巳 | 7/16 乙亥 |
| 三十 | | 3/21 戊寅 | | | 6/17 丙午 | 7/17 丙子 |

| 年紫白 | | | | | | | | | |
|---|---|---|---|---|---|---|---|---|---|
| | 3 | 8 | 1 | 男♂ ☴ 巽 | 會 | 運 | 世 | 年 | 23 |
| | 2 | 4 | 6 | 女♀ ☷ 坤 | 大過 | 姤 | 鼎 | 家人 | |
| | 7 | 9 | 5 | 元運 Duodecennial 8 | ䷛ | ䷫ | ䷱ | ䷤ | |

| 六月小 | 七月大 | 八月大 | 九月小 | 十月大 | 十一月小 | 十二月大 |
|---|---|---|---|---|---|---|
| 己未 | 庚申 | 辛酉 | 壬戌 | 癸亥 | 甲子 | 乙丑 |
| 3 | 2 | 1 | 9 | 8 | 7 | 6 |
| | | | | | | |
| 大暑 12 9:50 | 處暑 14 17:01 | 秋分 16 14:50 | 霜降 18 0:21 | 小雪 20 22:03 | 冬至 22 11:27 | 大寒 24 22:07 |
| 立秋 13 2:23 | 白露 15 5:27 | 寒露 17 21:16 | 立冬 19 0:35 | 大雪 21 17:33 | 小寒 23 4:49 | 立春 1 16:27 |
| | | | | | | |
| 7/18 丁丑 | 8/16 丙午 | 9/15 丙子 | 10/15 丙午 | 11/13 乙亥 | 12/13 乙巳 | 1/11 甲戌 |
| 7/19 戊寅 | 8/17 丁未 | 9/16 丁丑 | 10/16 丁未 | 11/14 丙子 | 12/14 丙午 | 1/12 乙亥 |
| 7/20 己卯 | 8/18 戊申 | 9/17 戊寅 | 10/17 戊申 | 11/15 丁丑 | 12/15 丁未 | 1/13 丙子 |
| 7/21 庚辰 | 8/19 己酉 | 9/18 己卯 | 10/18 己酉 | 11/16 戊寅 | 12/16 戊申 | 1/14 丁丑 |
| 7/22 辛巳 | 8/20 庚戌 | 9/19 庚辰 | 10/19 庚戌 | 11/17 己卯 | 12/17 己酉 | 1/15 戊寅 |
| 7/23 壬午 | 8/21 辛亥 | 9/20 辛巳 | 10/20 辛亥 | 11/18 庚辰 | 12/18 庚戌 | 1/16 己卯 |
| 7/24 癸未 | 8/22 壬子 | 9/21 壬午 | 10/21 壬子 | 11/19 辛巳 | 12/19 辛亥 | 1/17 庚辰 |
| 7/25 甲申 | 8/23 癸丑 | 9/22 癸未 | 10/22 癸丑 | 11/20 壬午 | 12/20 壬子 | 1/18 辛巳 |
| 7/26 乙酉 | 8/24 甲寅 | 9/23 甲申 | 10/23 甲寅 | 11/21 癸未 | 12/21 癸丑 | 1/19 壬午 |
| 7/27 丙戌 | 8/25 乙卯 | 9/24 乙酉 | 10/24 乙卯 | 11/22 甲申 | 12/22 甲寅 | 1/20 癸未 |
| 7/28 丁亥 | 8/26 丙辰 | 9/25 丙戌 | 10/25 丙辰 | 11/23 乙酉 | 12/23 乙卯 | 1/21 甲申 |
| 7/29 戊子 | 8/27 丁巳 | 9/26 丁亥 | 10/26 丁巳 | 11/24 丙戌 | 12/24 丙辰 | 1/22 乙酉 |
| 7/30 己丑 | 8/28 戊午 | 9/27 戊子 | 10/27 戊午 | 11/25 丁亥 | 12/25 丁巳 | 1/23 丙戌 |
| 7/31 庚寅 | 8/29 己未 | 9/28 己丑 | 10/28 己未 | 11/26 戊子 | 12/26 戊午 | 1/24 丁亥 |
| 8/1 辛卯 | 8/30 庚申 | 9/29 庚寅 | 10/29 庚申 | 11/27 己丑 | 12/27 己未 | 1/25 戊子 |
| 8/2 壬辰 | 8/31 辛酉 | 9/30 辛卯 | 10/30 辛酉 | 11/28 庚寅 | 12/28 庚申 | 1/26 己丑 |
| 8/3 癸巳 | 9/1 壬戌 | 10/1 壬辰 | 10/31 壬戌 | 11/29 辛卯 | 12/29 辛酉 | 1/27 庚寅 |
| 8/4 甲午 | 9/2 癸亥 | 10/2 癸巳 | 11/1 癸亥 | 11/30 壬辰 | 12/30 壬戌 | 1/28 辛卯 |
| 8/5 乙未 | 9/3 甲子 | 10/3 甲午 | 11/2 甲子 | 12/1 癸巳 | 12/31 癸亥 | 1/29 壬辰 |
| 8/6 丙申 | 9/4 乙丑 | 10/4 乙未 | 11/3 乙丑 | 12/2 甲午 | 1/1 甲子 | 1/30 癸巳 |
| 8/7 丁酉 | 9/5 丙寅 | 10/5 丙申 | 11/4 丙寅 | 12/3 乙未 | 1/2 乙丑 | 1/31 甲午 |
| 8/8 戊戌 | 9/6 丁卯 | 10/6 丁酉 | 11/5 丁卯 | 12/4 丙申 | 1/3 丙寅 | 2/1 乙未 |
| 8/9 己亥 | 9/7 戊辰 | 10/7 戊戌 | 11/6 戊辰 | 12/5 丁酉 | 1/4 丁卯 | 2/2 丙申 |
| 8/10 庚子 | 9/8 己巳 | 10/8 己亥 | 11/7 己巳 | 12/6 戊戌 | 1/5 戊辰 | 2/3 丁酉 |
| 8/11 辛丑 | 9/9 庚午 | 10/9 庚子 | 11/8 庚午 | 12/7 己亥 | 1/6 己巳 | 2/4 戊戌 |
| 8/12 壬寅 | 9/10 辛未 | 10/10 辛丑 | 11/9 辛未 | 12/8 庚子 | 1/7 庚午 | 2/5 己亥 |
| 8/13 癸卯 | 9/11 壬申 | 10/11 壬寅 | 11/10 壬申 | 12/9 辛丑 | 1/8 辛未 | 2/6 庚子 |
| 8/14 甲辰 | 9/12 癸酉 | 10/12 癸卯 | 11/11 癸酉 | 12/10 壬寅 | 1/9 壬申 | 2/7 辛丑 |
| 8/15 乙巳 | 9/13 甲戌 | 10/13 甲辰 | 11/12 甲戌 | 12/11 癸卯 | 1/10 癸酉 | 2/8 壬寅 |
| | 9/14 乙亥 | 10/14 乙巳 | | 12/12 甲辰 | | 2/9 癸卯 |

3rd Sexagenary Cycle

NOON
SUMMER
SOUTHERN FIRE
SE
SW
HORSE
SNAKE
SHEEP
FIRE
WATER
DRAGON
MONKEY
EASTERN WOOD
WESTERN METAL
SPRING
AUTUMN
RABBIT
METAL
ROOSTER
FIRE
TIGER
DOG
WOOD
EARTH
OX
RAT
PIG
NE
NW
NORTHERN WATER
WINTER
MIDNIGHT

# THE 22 ESSENTIAL CHARACTERS

## The Ten Heavenly Stems

| | | | | |
|---|---|---|---|---|
| 甲<br>Yang Wood<br>chia | 乙<br>Yin Wood<br>yi | 丙<br>Yang Fire<br>bing | 丁<br>Yin Fire<br>ding | 戊<br>Yang Earth<br>wu |
| 己<br>Yin Earth<br>ji | 庚<br>Yang Metal<br>geng | 辛<br>Yin Metal<br>sun | 壬<br>Yang Water<br>ren | 癸<br>Yin Water<br>gui |

| The Twelve Earthly Branches | | | | | |
|---|---|---|---|---|---|
| **Rat**<br>Yang Water<br>子<br>tze | **Ox**<br>Yin Earth<br>丑<br>chou | **Tiger**<br>Yang Wood<br>寅<br>yin | **Rabbit**<br>Yin Wood<br>卯<br>muw | **Dragon**<br>Yang Earth<br>辰<br>zhen | **Snake**<br>Yin Fire<br>巳<br>si |
| **Horse**<br>Yang Fire<br>午<br>wu | **Sheep**<br>Yin Earth<br>未<br>wei | **Monkey**<br>Yang Metal<br>申<br>shen | **Rooster**<br>Yin Metal<br>酉<br>yuw | **Dog**<br>Yin Metal<br>戌<br>su | **Pig**<br>Yin Water<br>亥<br>hai |

# About the Author

**Richard Ashworth**, one of the most respected Western Feng Shui Masters, is probably best known for his book *The Feng Shui Diaries* - an account of of a year of his life, including a term's study at Huazhong University in central China – as well as for introducing Classical Feng Shui to a mass audience on Channel Five's *HouseBusters*. He has studied with "every Chinese Master who'd give me the time of day" and performed perhaps a thousand feng shui surveys and drafted and interpreted several times that number of Ba Zis from Vancouver to Indonesia, Belgium to Australia.

He has worked with luminaries such as Kelly Hoppen, Gillian Anderson, Naomie Harris and many others "who didn't demand an NDA" as well as one or two who did. Unusually for an Englishman he has also addressed the Grand Masters at the International Feng Shui Conference in Singapore.

Ba Zi is, he says, a unique combination of natural laws not generally respected this side of the world, and pure divination; a hybrid of study and simple *qing*: the wish to make a positive difference. It is he says "the most powerful instrument of self-help" he has ever encountered.

Richard is married with six children and an ever-growing number of grandchildren and still spends most of his time teaching, consulting and practising Ba Zi and Feng Shui both live and via Zoom.

O-BOOKS

# SPIRITUALITY

**O is a symbol of the world, of oneness and unity; this eye represents knowledge and insight. We publish titles on general spirituality and living a spiritual life. We aim to inform and help you on your own journey in this life.**
**If you have enjoyed this book, why not tell other readers by posting a review on your preferred book site?**

## Recent bestsellers from O-Books are:

### Awakening Child

A journey of inner transformation through teaching your child mindfulness and compassion.
Heather Grace MacKenzie
Paperback: 978-1-78535-408-3 ebook: 978-1-78535-409-0

### A Colourful Dose of Optimism

Prescribe your own Happy Colours to Feel Good NOW
Jules Standish
It's time for us to look on the bright side, by boosting our mood and lifting our spirit, both in our interiors, as well as our closet.
Paperback: 978-1-78904-927-5 ebook: 978-1-78904-928-2

**Natural Happiness**

Use Organic Gardening Skills to Cultivate Yourself

Alan Heeks

Deepen your roots to grow through uncertainty.

Paperback: 978-1-80341-496-6 ebook: 978-1-80341-497-3

**Daylight Saving Time**

The Power of Growing Older

David W. Berner

Daylight Saving Time: Facing age with grace and mindfulness.

Paperback: 978-1-80341-511-6 ebook: 978-1-80341-520-8

**Generation Panic**

Simple & Empowering Techniques to Combat Anxiety

Agi Heale

Generation Panic is a one-stop shop with over 100 tips and techniques to help busy professionals combat anxiety.

Paperback: 978-1-78904-515-4 ebook: 978-1-78904-516-1

**Life Before the Internet**

What we can learn from the good old days

Michael Gentle

EA fascinating look back at a slower, simpler time, when Amazon was just a river.

Paperback: 978-1-80341-388-4 ebook: 978-1-80341-389-1

**Breath for Health**
A Mindful Way to Restore Your Natural Breathing Cycle
Michael D Hutchinson
Discover the secrets hidden in yoga and modern physiology — and restore your natural, healthy, confident way of breathing in just 10 minutes a day.
Paperback: 978-1-80341-440-9 ebook: 978-1-80341-441-6

Readers of ebooks can buy or view any of these bestsellers by clicking on the live link in the title. Most titles are published in paperback and as an ebook. Paperbacks are available in traditional bookshops. Both print and ebook formats are available online.

Find more titles and sign up to our readers' newsletter at
**www.o-books.com**

Follow O-Books on Facebook at **O-Books**

For video content, author interviews, and more, please subscribe to our YouTube channel:

**O-BOOKS Presents**

Follow us on social media for book news, promotions, and more:

**Facebook: O-Books**

**Instagram: @o_books_mbs**

**X: @obooks**

**Tik Tok: @ObooksMBS**

www.o-books.com